Future Pro(

How to keep yourself employable for the rest of your working career

by
David Yeabsley

Published by:
The Endless Bookcase
71 Castle Road, St Albans, Hertfordshire,
England UK, AL1 5DQ

Edited by:
Matt Noble Wright

Available from:
www.theendlessbookcase.com
Amazon, Kobo, Google and Nook.

Printed Edition:
Also available in multiple e-book formats.

ISBN: 978-1-912243-85-3

About David Yeabsley

David left school at 16 years old. His teachers never said about him, "He could try harder." He did try hard, very hard indeed, it's just that he wasn't very academic at school. Apart from sport that is — he was above average there, but he tried very hard at that too! If only he had had the skill to match his effort and enthusiasm, he could have been a professional sportsman.

Unfortunately, university wasn't an option for David, which was a shame — he would have loved to have gone; all that sport, that fun and all those experiences.

So, David went through several jobs after school and he always tried really hard. Some jobs he just didn't enjoy and some he just wasn't suited to, but he loved the experiences, the people and the challenges all the same.

Inspired by his grandmother (whom he firmly believes left this world with absolutely no regrets) he made a key decision and followed his passions. He set up his own training and coaching company helping people in businesses to maximise their potential. He has loved every minute of it and, over time, has become rather good at it.

He still prefers hands-on experience to academia and learning from life's experiences, and loves reading lots of books, attending numerous conferences and watching countless videos on self development and motivation.

David is great at learning from his own experiences and from those of other people whom he encounters. He puts maximum effort and enthusiasm into what he does and is extremely focused on making the right things happen.

This book is a reflection of his own learnings, thoughts, experiences and ideas and how David is working toward his own Future Proofing Journey.

Enjoy the journey of Future Proofing Yourself.

For more on David please see his:

Youtube Channel
https://www.youtube.com/user/MrYeabsley

LinkedIn Page
https://www.linkedin.com/in/davidyeabsley/

Websites
http://www.davidyeabsley.co.uk/
https://www.thepeopleanimators.com/

Contents

Introduction

This book is all about *you*. There is no *them* or *they* in this book. It's all about how *you* are going to look after *yourself* for the rest of your working career. Along the way, you will come to recognise your strengths. You will have honest conversations with yourself about the areas for personal improvement and development in order to keep yourself employable for the rest of your career.

So, ask yourself the question: "Do I invest enough time in my self-development?" Most of us will say "Not enough", and come up with various excuses and reasons as to why not.

These include excuses such as:

- I don't have time;
- I'm far too busy;
- My boss or company won't invest in me;
- I was going to but...

Today's working environment is becoming increasingly challenging and competitive. New technologies are being introduced so quickly into our working environments and daily lives, that by the time you will have read this page, somebody will have invented a new technology to make everything quicker and easier. So, are you keeping yourself up-to-date or are you being left behind?

Take a minute to reflect:

- What will your business and industry look like in the **next two to five years**? You may have plenty of skills and experience that you have gained over recent years, but will those skills still be relevant over the coming years?

- Are you able to **keep pace** with the relentless change in technology or are you already being left behind?
- Can you **remain relevant** to the younger generation? They think more than one step ahead and are full of new and innovative ideas to make our world turn faster and faster.

Like it or not, it's the new reality.

You need to ensure that you have the right skills, attributes, and mindset to keep yourself employable for however many working years you have left before retirement.

Whatever your dreams and aspirations are now, how are you going to pay for them all? The greatest investment you can make is in you. Your personal development, your skills and your mindset. You have made a great start in buying this book!

It is tough out there, but don't despair, help is at hand as long as you:

- Have a plan
- Can be honest with yourself
- Work hard
- Are totally motivated and organised
- Constantly learn and develop yourself
- Seek out new experiences and challenges
- Make the right decisions and choices
- Create the right future that best serves you

Procrastination is not an option though!

The greatest investment you can make is in you...in your personal development, your skills, and your mindset.

This book will help you develop all of those things.

Have you ever done any of the following?

Decided to be careful of what you eat or even decided to go on a diet?

Decided to do some exercise and get yourself fit by going to the gym, running, walking or fitness classes?

Tidied up or cleared out certain rooms in your house or undertaken a complete spring clean?

Decided it was time to get some financial planning advice, pensions, mortgages or decide to start budgeting?

Cleared out your old clothes and invested in a new wardrobe?

However, when was the last time that you sat down and thought about your self-development ? When was the last time you thought about how you are going to keep yourself employable and enjoy the rest of your working career?

Well, now is the time.

Woody and Buzz

The concept of 'Future Proofing Yourself' can be nicely demonstrated by the characters of the childrens' animation film *Toy Story* with the help of two of the key members of the cast, Woody and Buzz.

Woody was cast as the leading character... or so he thought. He was the best friend and trusted toy of a young boy called Andy. Woody was Andy's hero. They went everywhere together, fought battles together, travelled together on family outings; wherever Andy went, Woody also went. Woody would be by Andy's side whenever he needed him, for play or for comfort.

You could describe Woody's attributes as reliable, dependable and trustworthy, although he did have limited technical skills and his vocabulary wasn't much to shout about!

Andy had other toys, but they knew their place. Woody was Number One and all the other toys held him in high-esteem. They followed Woody and he was the leader and organiser in Andy's games. They were a great double act and partnership - Happy days!

Then suddenly one hot and sunny day, Woody's world fell apart. It was Andy's birthday and out of nowhere came a new toy called 'Buzz Lightyear'. Andy had never seen anything quite like Buzz before. It was love at first sight. Buzz was dynamic with new concepts and features like no other toy Andy possessed. With flashing lights and moveable parts, Buzz would take control of all situations with his commanding and self-assured presence. Plus, Buzz could shout, "To infinity and beyond". Andy didn't know where that was, but it sounded exciting and he was soon to find out. Buzz brought Andy new beginnings, new adventures and opportunities of excitement and fun.

But what about poor Woody? He had always been there for Andy, through thick and thin, but now he wasn't wanted, needed or desired anymore. His skills and attributes had become out-of-date, by just doing the same things he had become the 'same old, same old' Woody — he had become a routine in Andy's life.

By now Andy loved his new partner Buzz and they started out on new adventures; they went into space and of course, to infinity and beyond! Buzz could do anything and take Andy and his imagination anywhere they wanted to go.

Woody was reduced to just another toy in the playroom along with all the other toys. Then, as Andy became older, there was a real threat that they would all become redundant and disregarded. Packed off in boxes to charity shops or worse still to the dump! Something which they all worried about.

The truth is that, unfortunately, Woody hadn't 'Future Proofed' himself. He hadn't seen the day coming when his attributes and skills could become out-of-date. Woody's thinking, the way he communicated, the way he functioned and the way he worked had not moved with the times. He had become stale. He hadn't looked after himself — he was no longer needed and was of no value to Andy.

So, the serious point to this story is, "Are we all being pro-active and 'Future Proofing Ourselves'?"

Looking forwards, we will all probably have to keep working until we are older than our parent's generation, given the increased competition for our services, the squeeze on pensions and the happy prospect of increased life expectancy. So, there will still be time after retirement for cruises around the world and our own new adventures... but we will need to pay for it!

So how can we continue to represent an attractive proposition and a good investment for our clients and our employers?

We might have a wealth of experience and knowledge, but is it the right experience and knowledge our client's futures? Will people still want us around their businesses?

So, come on, let's all be Buzz Lightyears! Full of Buzz, let's inspire our own imagination and the imaginations of others... create new beginnings, take our clients on new adventures 'To Infinity and Beyond'... let's all go and Future Proof Ourselves with new skills and thinking.

Remember: if you don't look after yourself, who's going to do it for you?

We wouldn't want to all end up like Woody, would we?

Thank you – Have fun and enjoy the journey.

Chapter One: A Time to Reflect?

How will you make yourself employable and valuable to businesses for the rest of your career?

Will you have what they need?

Dad's story

Have you ever seen your Dad cry?

Have you ever seen your dad cry? Unfortunately, yes, I once did, and it had a huge impact upon my life.

I was sixteen and I was in the process of leaving school after completing my final GCSE exams. Arriving home from school one afternoon, I realised that my dad's car was parked in the driveway. This was strange, as he normally didn't arrive home from work until at least 6.30 pm. I went inside and my dad was sat in his chair, crying Something was very wrong; my dad was my rock – he never cried. I asked what was wrong?

He replied: "They don't need me anymore." "What do you mean?", I asked. "They don't need me anymore...they've made me redundant."

My dad was a very clever man and had worked as a scientist in the specialist metals industry since his apprenticeship almost 35 years ago. However, his position had become out-of-date and he never noticed the situation coming. Unfortunately, his skill set wasn't easily transferrable in such a specialist industry.

Straight after leaving school, I joined a large insurance company. It was like swapping one institution for another. I noticed that a lot people had been there for years and years, doing the same job, day in and day out. I could see what would happen to them, and in a few years, it did – the business relocated with wholescale redundancies. Many of the people I worked with ended up in a similar situation to my father, as they sought alternative employment with limited transferable skills.

Fortunately, with my dad's story very much in my mind, I had already left the insurance company by then, but I vowed that I would never let myself sleepwalk into the same predicament.

It took me several attempts to find the right job, and it wasn't until I turned 29 that I started working in business and skills training for motor and finance companies.

I soon realised that I was the only one who could look after my self-development, that only I could be responsible for my self-management, my future learning and my career development.

So, my question to everyone is: "What are you doing to manage your self-development?"

Will you look after you and invest in you? Please don't leave it to chance — constantly reflect, learn, and develop your skillset, your experiences and your knowledge.

*Only **you** can manage how to Future Proof Yourself.*

Future Proofing Yourself

What is it?

We are all individual commercial entities. We sell our knowledge, skills, ideas, time, expertise and wisdom to our employers in return for a salary and various other benefits.

We give up our personal time and sometimes put our general health and well-being to the test by working long hours in pressurised environments, trying to achieve corporate results.

However, all successful companies constantly develop new ideas, products and services for their customers. They employ people with the right skill sets and attributes to suit their objectives and to invest in new technologies and skills. They diversify before the market changes, remaining one step ahead (or if they are really good, two steps ahead) of the game with strategic thinking and excellent planning.

As individuals, do we do the same? Do we look after ourselves? Are our skills, experience, knowledge and thinking up-to-date? Do we sit back and analyse what our employers might demand in the future from us? Do we consider how the skills market is changing and what might be needed in the next 5 to 10 years?

Do we treat our employers and managers as customers and consider what do they need from us, now and in the future as their markets change?

Are we looking after ourselves, so that we are fit and strong enough to still be of value to our employers in the future and, in return, making ourselves employable for the rest of our careers?

If we don't look after ourselves, who is going to do it for us?

Welcome to Future Proofing Yourself

Who is this book for?

This book is for everyone. We are all going to feel vulnerable, in one way or another, at some time during our working careers. We might worry about the future of our company and our roles within them, or we might feel out of our depth and lacking in confidence. All these fears can now be managed — although everything might not always go the way we want, we can take control of our reaction to situations and make the right choices for us.

It is all about choices. However, we must make sure we put ourselves in the right position to manage those choices.

Ask yourself:

- If you are starting out in the big wide world or if you have been in the working environment for a few years: "What are your plans and aspirations?"
- If you have settled into your career and it is going well: "How are you going to keep on track...what's your plan?"
- If you encounter an unexpected nasty surprise or can foresee one on the horizon: "How will you bounce back... what's your plan?"

After all, if you don't look after yourself, who is going to do it for you?

Challenging and Uncomfortable

Future Proofing Yourself can be challenging and feel uncomfortable. However, now is not the time to put your head in the sand and hope it will all go away. Now is not the time to rely upon winning the lottery. This is a real issue.

There is no magic formula to Future Proofing Yourself – it is called self-management and professionalism.

Take somebody like Roger Federer, a tennis legend. He is a great professional who knows why he is so good so he can constantly perform to the best of his abilities. He gets paid lots of money so he should be professional and know what he is good at, shouldn't he? Well, we all think we are professional, so shouldn't we know what we are good at…shouldn't we be able to promote ourselves and constantly perform to the best of our abilities?

We will all have to operate outside of our comfort zone from time to time, to become involved in challenging and uncomfortable discussions which will require us to remain calm under pressure. We will need to learn new skills along the way which will not be natural to us and we will often feel out of our depth.

Future Proofing Yourself should be fun and involve new experiences, new people to talk with, new learning opportunities. It will help to develop your confidence, help you to achieve the right balance in life, help you to create new ways of thinking.

We may see people progressing quicker than us. Accept it all, embrace the challenge.

And above all help yourself to enjoy and feel valued and fulfilled in your journey.

Are you ready?

Your Working World

Let's take time to consider your working world and your long-term ambitions. What do you want to do and where do you want to go with it? Naturally, many of us will say 'Retire please', but that's not often a realistic option.

- Do we want to remain where we are, doing what we are currently doing — if so, do we have the right skill set and how might the market be changing?
- Do we want to progress in the role, develop in the business and move up a level — if so, what's our plan and how do we position ourselves? Plus, do we have the right skills and abilities?
- Do we want to change and do something completely different — if so, what? Do we want to retrain or just take our current skills and abilities and apply them elsewhere?
- Is going part-time or dropping down a level a possibility?

Do you have other things in life that you would like to do rather than just work? Ask yourself, realistically and financially, whether you are able to spend less time at work to do other purposeful, meaningful things in your life?

Celebrities and Sportspeople

We often hear stories of sportspeople who, as they approach the end of their careers, struggle with the fact they are no longer number one or the first choice on the team sheet. They miss the adulation, the crowds, the excitement, and the buzz of competition. The transition to normal life can be very challenging.

Actors also frequently struggle as they become of a mature age, with fewer roles on offer. Their past experiences and successes often count for nothing as they seek new parts in plays and films. Their agent stops phoning them. It can be a frustrating time.

Some are better than others in finding new ventures and careers, be it coaching/media within their sporting/acting world or something in a completely different industry altogether. Or they could just settle for a part on a reality television programme, often to the amusement of the general public!

Could you potentially suffer the same fate? Are your skills up-to-date? Do businesses value your knowledge, skills, ways of thinking and experiences? Do you, like the sports personalities and actors need to think about your future and focus upon how you can Future Proof Yourself?

Go and Reflect

Spend time talking to people you know. Sit down, reflect with a notebook and jot down all your ideas and thoughts. Then look back and reflect upon what you have written.

Who can you talk to?

- Go to Trade Shows; identify what type of work is out there.
- Talk to business contacts; go and visit their places of work.
- If you deal with customers, spend some more time understanding their business.

If you work in a large organisation:

- How do the different departments work?

- Do you really understand how it all works?
- Are there areas of opportunity for you internally?
- What can you learn to progress your career?

Also, on a personal level:

- What, other than work, would you like to do 'more of'?
- What are your hobbies, long-term plans, bucket lists?
- Where do you want to travel and who do you want to do it with?

Generate ideas, but don't evaluate them yet.

Sit down and think about activities outside of work which you would like to do 'more of'?

Again, generate ideas, write them down, but don't evaluate them yet. Hobbies, time with people, places to go, things to do...etc.

Where to reflect?

If you struggle to think and reflect at your desk, go and sit in a coffee shop, take a walk outside in the fresh air, or find venues and places that make you think differently.

Try reflecting when you travel, take a train journey and look out the window, gaze, daydream and allow your imagination to take you to somewhere new.

Think of places that inspire you: the seaside, sporting venues, churches, music venues, festivals, up a mountain!

Find whatever works best for you.

Who to reflect with?

Who makes you think differently?

Try and talk to people who are different to you — get them to explain how they see their world and what works or doesn't work for them. Listen and ask questions to help you understand their thought processes. They may come up with a gem of an idea that makes you think, "I like that, I could give it a go".

Turn your phone and devices off

Give your brain the space to think and don't let yourself be interrupted – turn those devices off!

Allow yourself time to invest in yourself. Find places that will permit you to change your thinking and give you time to reflect.

The Art of Reflection – Use a notebook

Take yourself, a pen and your notebook for a cup of tea and reflect. Power down your devices, switch your brain off from trying to absorb more information and try to find clarity in your thoughts, ideas, mind and your world.

Use the front of your notebook for your everyday lists of activities and tasks along with notes from conversations and meetings.

The back of your notebook should be used for reflection and thinking time. Add a few headings at the back to help you create direction and wellbeing for yourself.

The Art of Reflection is the key to Future Proofing Yourself. Future Proofing Yourself is all about creating the right skills, knowledge, experiences and wellbeing to keep yourself employable for the rest of your working career.

It's about taking control and thinking about your future choices.

Life is about Choices

Life is all about choices. Make sure you put yourself in the position to be able to have choices, to be able to make decisions that will benefit you and your family.

I do appreciate that life often prevents us from having choices; for example when we are dealt a difficult hand in terms of health and the unexpected. However, most of us do have choices, but are we willing to take responsibility for those choices instead of waiting for things to happen?

One of my favourite sayings is,"If in doubt give it a go." This is because you will always learn from the experience, which will give you the opportunity to have more choices in life. By trying new things you will discover what you like, but just as importantly, what you don't like. This is the problem a lot of people have in terms of career choice, especially when young and starting out — they are not sure what they want to do? It is often easier to work out what you don't want to do and go from there.

The more skills and experiences you have, the more naturally you will unearth opportunities and the greater your career choices will be. So, put the effort in at the outset and you will be rewarded further down the line.

The more effort you put into a career choice or passion, the more opportunities you will have.

In sales, the more people you speak to, the more opportunities people have to say "Yes". However, if you only speak to only a few people, you have less chance of people saying "Yes", which naturally reduces your opportunities. This is the same as exploring new work opportunities – the more people you speak to, the more chance something will come up.

I have been coaching an aspiring young actor who is finding it tough to get a break and to follow his passion. He currently spends a few hours each day looking at acting roles on different websites, but this hasn't really brought him much work. We brainstormed other avenues which could generate exposure and hence work opportunities: blogs, YouTube, open mic events, festivals for actors, writing scripts, running school drama sessions, compering and hosting at charity events radio shows, hosting quiz nights...etc.

When I asked him whether he had looked at all these avenues and really given his passion and acting career a good go, his answer was, "No, I get up too late." I replied: "Well, it's your choice what time you get up and it's your choice whether to do these activities which could bring more opportunities."

Just don't in a few years' time, regret not giving your passion and desired career a really good go, because you ended up doing something that you don't really want to do. Too many people say, "I was going to do that...if only I had."

Create your choices —most of us have a choice in what we eat, how we exercise, what we spend our money on, and what we do with our time.

Take control of your choices.

Do you have a clear idea of how you want your career to plan out?

Not many people do. Creating thinking time and talking with a good network of people can help you ask and answer lots of questions, but it requires effort and energy — you need to be enthusiastic about *you*.

What is your vision for *you* and *your* plan?

You wouldn't want to work for a company that had no vision and no strategy on how to achieve that vision, would you? Those types of companies don't survive just going from day to day. Remember you are a limited company, be a good one.

No more *Them* and *They* - it is down to *Me* now

Them and *They* - these are great words to ban from your vocabulary. We often find ourselves waiting for *them* or *they* to do something for us or blaming *them* and *they* for not doing the things that we thought they should have done. If we always wait for others to do things for us, it could become rather a long wait.

We often want others to change, rather than seeking change in ourselves.

There is a line in the song *Man in the Mirror* which goes: "I am asking him to change his ways." Have a listen to the lyrics — they are very inspiring and help us to see that we can make changes first.

Another great song is Paloma Faith or Mama Cass Elliott - *Make Your Own Kind of Music.*

Who are this *them* or *they*? Don't blame others for things over which you have no control.

Think about what *I, Me* and *We* can do. Take control of situations and pursue your own opportunities and choices.

In summary, don't spend your time and energy worrying about *them* and *they* —put that energy into what you can do for *you* and the people that matter to *you.*

But I don't have time

Once a week, I arrive home and my wife asks me, "Have you phoned your sister yet?" — I hope she doesn't read this! — and I usually reply, "No, I haven't had time yet."

However, if I were to arrive home one night and my wife were to say: " Your sister phoned – she's just won £6.8 million on the lottery, can you call her?"

Well I guess I might just find time to do that!

It's not that we don't have time to do things — we all have the same 168 hours a week— it's just that we have chosen to do other things instead. So, just be honest with yourself and others. If it's important, do it — if it isn't, don't.

Right now, where's my sisters' number?

A good starting point

Let's take a simple starting point — what areas of self-development do you need to work on? Think of feedback from within your working environment (managers, colleagues, team members, clients) as well as personal situations outside of work.

What are your strengths and what do you need to develop?

- People Skills
- Technical and IT Skills
- Management Skills

- Networking Skills
- Self-Confidence
- Self-Motivation
- Positive Thinking
- Communication and impact on others
- Resilience
- Calmness
- Drive
- Personal interests / hobbies

Are there any other threats to your development?

Great questions to reflect on when *Future Proofing Yourself*

Grab a cup of tea or coffee, turn off your devices, and invest in some one-on-one time with yourself to just think, ponder, and reflect. Some of these questions will be more relevant than others, so just move on to the ones that you feel are best-suited to your personal situation.

- If you don't look after yourself, who will?
- What do you enjoy the most about your work?
- What don't you enjoy about your work?
- What are your natural strengths?
- What are you passionate about?

- What hidden talents do you have that you feel are underutilised?
- What's your definition of success?
- What would you like to create / develop for yourself and those closest to you?
- What would you describe as your biggest weakness?
- What advice would you give someone in the same situation as you to help develop their potential and maximise opportunities that are put before them?
- How can you take more self-responsibility in managing your own appraisal and Personal Development Reviews (PDRs) / development plans in the future?
- Would you want to work with you? And why?
- If you have management responsibilities, would you want *you* as your manager? And why?

Inside Me

What are my passions?

Knowing what really makes you tick and being able to follow your passions in your career can be achievable. I was once asked by a senior IT Director: "Should I enjoy my job? And do people you meet enjoy their jobs?" He clearly didn't, which was why he lacked motivation and passion for his work, hence the reason for the coaching course. Knowing what your passions are and what excites you is vital to building a long and happy career.

Take a minute to reflect and think about the following questions to start giving yourself some direction:

- What are the passions that motivate me to do what I do. Or, to put it more frankly, if I didn't get paid for it, would I still be interested in doing it?
- What do I love about my job, and what (if anything) is missing?
- What makes me tick, what gives me a buzz?
- Do I want new challenges or would I prefer to stay in my comfort zone?
- What are my values and how can they point me in the right direction?
- What is important to me as a person (what makes me who I am)?

This exercise isn't everybody's cup of tea, but it's a good one to get started. Remember, none of this is right and none of it is wrong – it's all about you and what is right for you.

So, please don't sit around and read this thinking, "I should be doing this", or "I should have done that." Also, don't start comparing yourselves with others - be yourself and do what is right for you, make the right choices and decisions for you and those that you care for

However, be aware of those choices and manage and control them — don't look back in regret and think, "I should have done this..." or "I should have done that..." and "Only, if only!" Regret is very hard to revisit and put right.

One last thing: whilst you are thinking, or reflecting or talking with others, do keep a record and write everything down in order to understand your thought process; use a notebook or create a file on your device or laptop.

Remember, this is an investment in you.

What makes me happy?

What makes me happy? It's a question we often think about, but do we really ever answer it? Spend time writing down what inspires you, what makes you feel good about yourself and what you enjoy the most. Is there a connection between what makes you happy and your work? If there is, then that's a great sign of success.

Get some feedback

Start with yourself — look in the mirror and ask your reflection:

- Would you want you as your manager (if you are a manager)?
- Would you want you in your team (if you work with others in a team)?
- Would you want you as a friend?
- Would you want you as a parent?
- Would you want you as a brother or a sister?

Think about your responses. Do you need to be more aware of the impact that you have on others? What behaviours do you need to adapt, develop or even change?

So then start to ask others for feedback

Take time to solicit feedback from others on your strengths and weaknesses. Perhaps most importantly, are there any other areas where people feel you might be better suited given your qualities?

Ask:

1. Your team at work
2. Your colleagues
3. Your peer groups at work
4. Your manager or other managers you work with
5. Your partner
6. Your friends
7. Your family at home

Listen to their responses

- Don't get defensive
- Ask for examples
- Acknowledge what you feel is true
- Ask how they think you could change
- Thank them and action what you need to action

But don't stop being you!

Feedback is an essential mechanism to help us develop and grow. Professional sportspeople are constantly receiving feedback on what they do well and what they need to improve upon. They embrace feedback so they can develop and be the best they can possibly be. If we like to think of ourselves as professional, don't we owe it ourselves to seek out feedback so we can become better versions of ourselves?

Honest feedback can be life-changing

When I left school, I went to work for a large insurance company helping to write financial planning reports for potential investors. The job was ok and interesting in parts, but I must say that, on the whole, it was often more than a bit boring.

As ever, I always tried hard, always turned up on time, and never took sick days. However, having to sit in an office and concentrate was never one of my strong points. Often, after lunch, I would go for a walkaround the offices thinking of ways to pass the afternoon hours and catching up with my friends across all the different departments. The old 'walking-around-offices-holding-a-piece-of-paper-routine'... looking busy!

So, fast-forward to the good old annual appraisal time. My poor manager who was responsible for getting me to focus had the job of giving me some harsh but very fair feedback, it went something like this:

"We like having you in the office David, you are good fun to have about. Let's say your work is, well, satisfactory, but you must be the biggest pain up the backside I have ever had to manage. Please could you go and find another job?"

My manager was right, I just wasn't suitable for that type of work.

Now I'm not sure I would recommend that style of feedback in today's environment, but it worked. I left, went traveling, tried more than a few jobs when I returned, until eventually I found something that I loved, enjoyed, and was eventually good at.

Since then, as a manager myself, I have had several conversations with team members along the lines of, "What is it that you would really like to do for a job, career...etc?" Sometimes the tough feedback is the best – learn from it, act on it, and don't get defensive about it, especially if it carries an uncomfortable but very valid point.

Chapter Two: Personal Development and Maximising Opportunities

If in Doubt, Go for It

Life is a journey

Live it well
Enjoy the adventure
Be curious and ask lots of questions
Grab experiences and adventures
Be confident and know your strengths
Be the best you
Be good at what you do
Reflect and plan
Don't let unexpected surprises catch you out
Share and help others
Listen and understand
Enjoy and have fun
Share your wisdom and learn from others
Decide that procrastination doesn't exist
You have won the lottery, but you just don't know it yet

Future Proof Yourself
and
inspire others to do the same

Who is responsible for your personal development? And how much time should you allocate to it?

It is essential that we invest in ourselves and in our future career prospects... in the same way that we should take financial precautions to protect ourselves and our families during our working lives and through to retirement.

At least twice a year, you should sit down and reflect upon the relevant skills, knowledge and experience necessary to undertake your job. If you are looking to progress further, ask yourself what new skills, knowledge and experiences you might need to develop for the future? To simply stand still and carrying on doing the same job, you will need to develop and learn new ways of working to keep your skills up-to-date and hence, to ensure you remain employable.

We are starting to realise that change is 'the new normal'. New technology, new ways of thinking and new ways of working with a younger generation are all impacting upon our working environment. So how well are we adapting and changing in order to keep ourselves relevant?

In our working environment and in our lives in general, we keep trying to pack more and more into every single day in order to accomplish more and more. There is a constant pressure to keep achieving and performing. We are constantly challenging our bodies to be on 'full go' all the time and to be constantly winning.

So, even more reason to press the pause button and sit down and reflect. Are we looking after ourselves, are we going in the right direction and are we making the right choices in our careers so we can be employable and of value for the rest of our working day?

Reflection time is essential. We need to factor it into our lives, to take time to stop, think, reflect. We need to make the right choices for ourselves, given our current situations and circumstances. We need to afford ourselves opportunities and choices by improving our skills, knowledge and experiences and in turn, our learning and development.

Life is all about choices. However, we need to put ourselves in the position to make those choices, so we are not reliant upon others to make them for us.

Deciding upon your career direction will be a very significant and (usually) difficult choice. Remember that you will have to spend a lot of time at work, so you will need to examine your passions and what you enjoy doing, what career best matches your skill-set.

Having healthy career aspirations will create drive, enthusiasm and motivation — it will help you to maximise your potential. Developing ideas and plans for your career will naturally help you make the right choices in terms of what skills, knowledge and experiences will be needed both now and for your future. Building a good network of contacts will also help you to look at the choices and what alternatives are available. We will all need help, so building a healthy network of good contacts can save you a lot of time and energy in making the right choices.

A key area of Future Proofing Yourself is understanding what motivates you and how to stay motivated. Knowing how to get the best out of yourself will help you maximise your potential and work to the best of your abilities. When you are faced with challenges and setbacks, knowing your motivation values will help you to self-manage the situation and turn a difficult time or situation around so you can still perform to the best of your abilities.

Love life and love learning. Never stop learning or taking on new experiences — if you don't do this for yourself, then who is going to do it for you? Build opportunities to learn; most of us learn best by having new experiences, so go out and grab lots of experiences! Learn to work outside your comfort zone and to embrace new challenges. Learn from other people in your network and from their experiences, learn how your business works and how your clients' businesses work.

If in doubt, go out of your comfort zone and try new things. Only you can do this for yourself. Go and be inquisitive, ask more questions and learn more. We were always encouraged to do this as children and if you have children, I dare say you encourage them to always be learning and try new things. So why when we become adults, do we stop this way of thinking?

The Annual Appraisal. So many people dread this in the corporate world and they are often not run very well. If your manager isn't very good at them, do it for yourself. Create that thinking and reflection time at least twice a year and reflect upon how well you are managing your skills, knowledge and experiences. Get job descriptions for your current role and the future roles that you aspire to. What might you need to develop in terms of skills, knowledge and experience to keep your current job and what might you need to do to progress and take on new roles and opportunities?

If you don't do it for yourself, who is going to do it for you?

The Art of Reflection

Not taking the phone to London

I recently spent a business day in London without my phone (not by choice, but that's another story!)

So how did I cope?

Well, I spent more time reading my coaching notes and preparing for my meetings and coaching sessions.

I can honestly say I was fully prepared and didn't sit in client reception areas looking at my phone. Instead, I focused on what I needed to achieve. I looked genuinely pleased to see the people I was meeting instead of being distracted by my phone as I hurriedly completed an email or text (it's amazing how many times you see that and yes, I have been guilty!)

I was therefore always present, engaged and focused. I ate my lunch, not looking at my phone but thinking, reflecting, contemplating and enjoying the moment. I even had time to smile at the chap opposite with his laptop open, two phones on the go, and an egg and cress sandwich falling apart down his suit (something that has probably happened to us all at one point or another!)

I finished my lunch mulling over a few ideas that I have been meaning to think about for a while. I noticed that as soon as I had finished my meetings, I didn't rush to look at my phone or check my emails whilst walking down the road. I felt liberated by the opportunity to think and to savour the moment before indulging in my favorite hobby of people-watching.

I sat on the train, got out my notebook, reflected some more, and organised my thoughts, plans and ideas. I was free to think. Would I do it again? Yes and no. Naturally, it's vital that we remain contactable and are able to get things done on-the-go. However, it was great to be able to spend the day not tied to my phone and to allow myself time to think, daydream (another great pastime) and simply to enjoy the moment. So, after a rather pleasant snooze, I arrived home, chilled and relaxed.

Did I miss not having my phone on me? The only real downside was that I didn't receive my daughter's text about buying her some hair-straightening gel, so she wasn't too happy with me. However, that did save me some money... and she soon got over it!

When I did finally get around to looking at my emails, the world hadn't stopped turning, there was still oxygen in the air and running water on tap. So, happy days; enjoy it and give it a go— have a phone-free day!

Reflection time is a very underutilised activity; I guess we just don't have time for it anymore?! We are always worrying about what we think we should be doing rather than enjoying the moment. Finding time and space to think is becoming increasingly tough in today's environment where everything is accessible 24/7.

Using a notebook

In today's digital age, the one item that has seemed to survive unchanged is the good old trusty notebook; many people still use them to make 'To Do' lists or to take down notes from meetings. A notebook can be a very valuable tool in *Future Proofing Yourself* – use it to reflect on the key questions that we will cover throughout this book:

Consider having a few pages at the back of your notebook that you can reflect upon; I've listed a few examples below:

- What Personal Goals would I like to achieve?
- What are my Values? Which ones are important to me and which do I need to focus on?
- What have I learnt and how am I developing?
- What are my passions and what am I good at?
- Who would I like to have in my network of contacts?
- My Great Ideas [draw these as a mind map].
- What is really important to me and what makes me happy?
- What should I be thankful for?
- What has gone well and what have I enjoyed?

Use your notebook as a reflection tool to encourage yourself to reflect, think positively and try the following tips. You may prefer to record your thoughts on your phone or other mobile devices, but do try to switch off the applications that can interrupt you when reflecting:

- When you are traveling turn your phone off.
- Look out of the window and daydream.
- Go and have a cup of tea or coffee with yourself.
- Turn the telly off in the evening.
- Put on some inspiring music.
- Go walking and sit outside — find a favourite thinking spot.
- Create ideas and thoughts you might enjoy.

There was a great advert I noticed on a train recently; "When was the last time you were totally absorbed in a social media post?" Exactly! Turn it off and create some positive thoughts for yourself!

Daydreaming

I love daydreaming. In fact, I think it should be an essential life skill which is taught to everybody!

Select a comfy chair, lie on your bed, or sit outside on the grass, and clear your brain. Think of something you like to do and just let your mind go where it wants to go... if you have any negative thoughts, tell them to take a hike!

Turn your phone off and savour the moment.

Ask yourself silly questions. If you are people-watching in a coffee shop, ask yourself random or hypothetical questions:

- Where are they going? Where would I like to be going?
- Why are they in such a rush? Do I rush too much... and if so, why?
- I wonder why they chose that particular coffee or meal? What would I have chosen instead?
- Where might they live? What would be my ideal place to live?

Give your brain a rest and daydream – just keep things simple.

Aspirations for your career

Do you have a clear direction of what you want to do and why you want to do it? If you do, that's great — that's half the battle in being successful and enjoying work. However, if you don't and are unsure of your direction, then now is the time to sit down, to plan, and to create the right career path for yourself.

Go back to page 2 and ask yourself: "Where do I need to develop and create plans in order to achieve my development and career aspirations?"

I often work with young adults who are either leaving education or are new to the working environment and are unsure about what they want to do or in which direction they want to go.

I ask them what they think they are good at, what do they enjoy, what skills and attributes do they possess which could help them in certain working environments? What are their passions which could inspire them towards a career?

Often, they are just not sure of what direction to go in, so it's as much a case of working out what they don't want to do, as much as finding out what they do want to do. I encourage them to talk to family and friends to find out what they do and what they enjoy and don't enjoy. Is there someone else that they know doing something that they find interesting? Go to job fairs, talk to as many people as possible to gain ideas and learn from other people's experiences.

No matter where you are in your career, it's good to talk to people in your network to find out what they do or how their company works in order to generate ideas for your self-development.

Have you ever spent time in another company seeing what they do? Look at opportunities to do so to help expand your horizons and see other working environments to inspire you on your career selections and aspirations.

It is true that taking a new career path can be difficult, as you will probably lack the requisite skills and experience at the outset and may not be able to immediately earn what you were previously earning.

However, remember how many more years you might still have left in your working life. Do you want to look back when you retire and think, "I'm glad I spent all that time not enjoying myself", or, "That was good — it was tough at times, but I think I made the right choices"?

What motivates you?

Having a clear understanding of what motivates you is essential to getting the most out of your job and from life in general. This will be closely linked with your values, so it is a good idea to look at those values whilst considering the question of your motivation.

All human beings like to feel valued. Older people have the benefit of wisdom and experience – when we ask for their opinion and listen to them, they feel valued. At the other end of the spectrum, very young children love it when we listen to their ideas and stories — when they have our attention, they too feel valued. In fact everybody, regardless of age, likes to feel valued and appreciated.

Self-value is very important. Everybody has different motivating values depending upon their age, the different situations they have experienced through life and their own circumstances. Different motivating values could include job satisfaction, doing new things, coming out of a comfort zone, staying in a comfort zone, having targets, opportunities to learn, working in a team, working by oneself, helping others, being in control of one's own destiny. The list goes on.

When we are having a bad day or feeling unmotivated, what gets us going again? Is it talking to others, self-talk, music, going to different environments to think?

Spend time reflecting and thinking to yourself, "What makes me tick?"

Being demotivated isn't much fun. Working out your motivating values is important for your wellbeing, allowing you to perform to the best of your abilities and Future Proof Yourself.

Spend more time thinking about what you really want to do and what makes you feel good about yourself — you may have to work at it in order to work it out.

The concepts in this book take practice and effort. Change doesn't just happen overnight – you have to make it happen. You can't expect others to do it for you, or blame them because you haven't put the effort in.

Does money motivate you? Before you say, "Yes that's my motivation – lots of money please!", picture the following scenario. Imagine if I were to offer to treble your wages, but in return you would have to sit in a room for 9 hours a day, writing a report on how the light changes the colour of the room. Without any human interaction or access to digital devices, how long do you think you could last?

Money is, of course, important. Everybody likes money, but are you prepared to work harder, to study more for new qualifications, to add more value to the organisation you work for or take on more responsibility? To earn more money when you are working for someone else, you have to demonstrate that you can add more value to the people paying your wages.

So, we would like more money, but we would also like a decent work:life balance — what would that look like for you? Think about it.

Your Motivation Contract with yourself

What is your Motivation Contact with yourself? What I mean by this is, what are you prepared to put into your work and what would you like out of it in return?

I call this the Scales of Motivation.

Below is an example of my Scales of Motivation:

What am I prepared to put in to my work?	**What do I want out of my work?**
Energy	Money
Knowledge	Career
Skills	New Learning
Health	Job satisfaction
Family time	Being part of a team
Personal time	Security
Energy	Work:life balance
Experience	Challenges
Support	Opportunities
Dedication	A purpose
Loyalty	Being valued
Honesty	Holidays

Everybody is unique, so I expect your list will be somewhat different to mine. Spend some time thinking about whether your Scales of Motivation balance or whether you need to make some changes.

As you go through life, your scales will hopefully balance out. However, there will be times when you find yourself putting more in than you are getting out. This can lead to demotivation which is never a good thing.

Are you prepared to send and answer emails late at night, make calls at a weekend, work hours of unpaid overtime? Sometimes the answer will be "Yes", because you are receiving something back in return, be it experience, exposure, respect, or job satisfaction.

However, if over long periods of time you feel that the balance is not right, you need to take control and make changes.

Be aware of what it is and try and make the right choices to manage your career accordingly.

Being on a what I call a 'career bender' is fine; i.e. working all hours and giving your job everything. However, you need to make sure it is for the right reasons and there is either a purpose to it all, or a specific goal that you are working towards.

On the other hand, you might wish to work as little as possible, remaining safe in your comfort zone. However, ask yourself how long you can keep this up for? We all have to keep learning new skills and dealing with change to stay employed. Will you possess the relevant skills to keep yourself employable?

Personal Values and Self-Motivation

Take time out and think about some of the questions below and challenge yourself to reflect upon your answers. We all want to feel valued but there are a lot of other motivating values besides 'feeling valued'. What are yours?

Ask yourself:

- What is really important to you as a person?
- What personal values are important to you?
- What gives you real purpose and meaning and makes you feel fulfilled and good about yourself?
- What really motivates you? (This will change over time, but if you have just written down "Money", then try to think a little deeper.)
- What is your personal mission in life?
- Where do you see yourself in 3, 5, and 10 years' time?
- What are the first steps you need to take to get yourself there?

Job Security – is it important to you?

Job security is important for everyone — I don't think many people would argue against that. But where do we find job security in today's current working environment?

We can work for a good company where people will always need our service or products, but as we know, the unexpected should always be planned for. As discussed elsewhere in this book, markets change fast and technology can change even faster in our working environments.

Like it or not, the only place you can achieve true job security is through your own skills, talent and how you manage your personal development. So, if job security is important to you, keep reading and make your personal development a key priority for your future.

Motivation – working on your own v working in a team

When thinking about career and job choices, do consider whether you prefer working in a team environment or on your own. Are you motivated by the successes of the team, the buzz of working alongside others, the banter and the support of a group, or do you prefer working on your own, making your own decisions and being in sole control?

It is important to establish this so that you can make the right career choices and remain motivated in your career.

I was recently coaching a gentleman who wanted to progress into a management role— he saw this as the only way to progress his career. However, this person then proceeded to tell me: "I would like to be the manager of a team, but I do get very frustrated when people don't do what I want and don't take on my ideas. I normally find most people can't do it as well as me."

After a chatting further, we agreed that being in a team and managing people probably wasn't the best career path for him, and that a better option would be to position himself as a technical expert in a project management role where he didn't have to rely on other people too heavily. So, give this some serious thought.

Opportunities to Learn and Develop

A lifelong approach to your career development is essential for your future wellbeing and success.

My aunty learnt how to use her first computer at the age of 91 when we helped her buy her first iPad. She could then Skype her family in Australia and we could also send her emails with pictures attached to keep her up-to-date with all the things that we are doing. She even used Google to look up information. She did once ask what else she could find on Google... we just smiled and told her to be careful and to stick to the BBC websites!

Our businesses and our everyday worlds are constantly changing, so we have to try and stay one step ahead of the game by constantly learning and developing. We have no choice but to keep adapting and learning as change becomes the new normal.

There are two ways to think about the challenge of constantly learning and adapting: one is to keep our technical skills up-to-date, whilst the other is to keep our non-technical skills relevant.

Many people have told me during coaching sessions that they have plenty of years of experience, knowledge and skills. My next question to them is, "Yes but do you have the **right** experience, knowledge and skills for your business and industry for the up-and-coming years? Are you still relevant? How are you going to keep yourself relevant and adding value to the companies that you want to employ you?"

Technical Skills

Ask yourself:

- What technical skills do I have which are relevant?
- What technical skills do I need to keep up-to-date?

- What is my plan for managing these technical skills?
- What do I think my business and industry will look like in the near future and in the next few years?
- What major changes will I have to adapt to?
- What new technical skills or ways of thinking might come into play?
- Might I have to retrain or change industry at some stage?

Constantly reviewing your technical skills in your chosen market or industry is essential to preventing nasty surprises. Please remember my father's story from earlier in the book — I am sure we all know someone who has suffered a similar fate. It is always easier to stay in our comfort zone and to just carry on with our careers, but it is essential to always keep one eye on the future.

It is fair to say that nowadays we need to keep developing and learning just to stand still. I appreciate this will differ in different industries and job roles, but please don't become complacent and don't procrastinate. Procrastination is a great way to step back from your responsibilities of Future Proofing Yourself.

Behaviours – Capabilities – Beliefs

Thinking and reflecting on your Behaviours, Capabilities, and Beliefs will help you to determine whether you are making the right impact on yourself and the people with whom you work. It is good to be yourself but becoming self-aware of how you interact and impact upon others will be very helpful when it comes to managing yourself.

To get yourself thinking, try some of the questions below as you read through this chapter:

Behaviours

- What changes do you need to make in your behaviours?
- What habits do you think might hold you back?
- What new behaviours would you like to develop?
- What reactions do you notice in others when you interact with them that cause you concern?
- What will others see/hear/feel when after you have made changes in your behaviour?

Capabilities

- What capabilities do you want to change?
- Which skills and capabilities are you currently using?
- Do you have any skills or capabilities that are under-utilised?
- What do you need to do more of?

Beliefs

- What beliefs do you want to have about yourself?
- What do you currently believe about yourself?
- What beliefs are important to you?
- Which beliefs do you feel are positive and which do you believe are negative?
- How will you need to believe in yourself to make changes happen?
- What values will you need to draw on to change the beliefs you have now?

Non-Technical Skills

Your non-technical skills are perhaps best described as your ability to apply your technical skills in your working environment. In other words, how you communicate, influence, negotiate and manage situations.

We can all be technically brilliant in our field of expertise, but we need to get our message across to other people in a way that they can understand so that they can buy into our ideas.

Having excellent non-technical skills can be almost as important as your technical skills if you have to work across your business with non-technical people.

So how do humans learn? The key factor is by living, doing, and gaining new experiences. The more experience you have, the more opportunities you have to learn, so go out and grab an experience!

How quickly can you answer the following questions?

- What have you learnt about yourself recently?
- What new experiences have you taken on?

If you take rather a long time to think of some answers or, worse still, can't think of anything at all, I would suggest that you lack self-awareness when it comes to managing your learning and development. It is essential that you ask yourself the two questions above on a regular basis. Every day, you undergo new experiences, be they from challenges, conversations, or new environments. You need to always be asking yourself, "What am I learning?" Should your answer be "Nothing", then I suggest that you need to get out more. We can always be learning – by embracing a lifetime of learning, you will enjoy life more, gain new confidence and importantly it will help you to Future Proof Yourself.

Take a notebook, head up a page with "What have I learnt?", and reflect on this from time to time. Do it more regularly if you are new to a job or are going through a period of new challenges which provides you with the opportunity to take on new experiences.

Self-coaching to learn more

After meetings, presentations, challenging conversations, or projects, practice some of the following questions. Create some reflection time. Don't be too hard on yourself – try to remain honest and objective.

- What did I learn?
- What went well?
- What could I have done better?
- What other opportunities are there coming up to apply the learning?
- What could I learn from others?

Other opportunities to learn – Books, Films, Videos, Podcasts

Create a list again in the back of your notebook or create a new document on your device. Every time you talk to someone and they mention a new book, film, podcast, or YouTube video, write it down and check it out. It's a great way to motivate yourself to keep learning.

Challenge yourself to read a new book or watch a new film on a regular basis. Create your own library and lists of favourites. I still buy my books and films as I prefer a physical library, but you may prefer to access them on your mobile device — do whatever works best for you.

Getting into the habit of reading quality articles by industry experts, LinkedIn blogs (other networking sites are available!) and share them with people who you know are interested in the same topics. This is a good way to network and raise your profile in a subtle way, but don't go over the top, otherwise people will wonder if you ever do any work?!

Conferences and Webinars

Are you keeping yourself up-to-date with new ideas from conferences and webinars? Ask yourself which ones should you be dialling in to or attending?

Company training courses are brilliant (they keep people like me in a job!), but if you are invited to attend one, do make sure that you know why you are going and what you want to get out of it. If your manager recommends that you go, then feel free ask why— "What do you want me to take from the course?" Do make sure your manager schedules a follow-up with you. Keep your action plans from your courses and review them at your Appraisals and Personal Development Reviews (PDRs).

One-to-One Coaching and Mentoring Sessions

If you get offered any one-to-one coaching or mentoring sessions, you would be mad to pass them up. Do make sure you go in with some clear goals of what you would like from the sessions in order to maximise the opportunity and the learning. Have some great questions to ask and keep an open mind on what is discussed. Take your notebook with you, make notes, and create clear action plans. Use the topics in this book to ask questions and be curious about other people's thoughts and ideas. It's free information and free learning, so grab it and be proactive and positive towards the experience.

Go grab an experience

Love Life – Love Learning. Life is for learning so go grab an experience.

Do you know anyone who is wise? Hopefully one day, my children will say "My Mum and Dad"... we can but live in hope! Often people whom we perceive as wise have had a wealth of lifetime experiences. However, more importantly, they have learned from those experiences. I appreciate that it's a very simple concept, but the more experiences you have in life, more chance you have of becoming wise and able to make the right choices and decisions based on those experiences.

So, it's time to get out there and grab some experiences.

Here's another page for your notebook: "What do I need to learn and what new experiences do I need to gain?"

Create a list of opportunities to gain new experiences inside and outside your workplace:

Inside work	**Outside work**
Meetings	Travel
New conversations	New Hobbies
Presentations	Sporting challenges
Time with senior managers	Theatre – Concerts
Different parts of the business	New places to visit
New projects	New Friends
Secondments	Sporting events
Cross team working	Talks and shows
New clients	New people to talk to

Go grab an experience. If in doubt, just give it a go – you will always learn something from it.

Lifelong learning is a choice, a way of life. Plan time for learning, whether to keep yourself employable, and of value to your business, or to make yourself more marketable in your industry.

I am getting paid for this and so can you

I have had the wonderful opportunity to work with lots of different organisations in different sectors, environments and countries. What I love most about my job is that I am always learning from these different organisations, and yes, I do get paid for working with them.

But what I truly love is working with entrepreneurs and family-run businesses that have grown and developed over the years. I love to talk with the people who have been instrumental in the ideas and development of a business and its success. I spend time understanding their story, how they made their decisions, what they did in tough and crucial times, how they see their future, their plans, and passions. And yes, I still get paid for learning.

So, wherever possible, make sure you always take up the opportunity to talk to other businesses, show an interest and to inquisitive about the people you meet every day in your professional life. And, if you are good at your job, the experience will enrich you and you, like me, will be getting paid for learning. Can't be bad. Getting paid for learning is even better than learning for free, isn't it?

Memberships, Accreditations, Trade Organisations

Which memberships, accreditations, or trade organisations might be the best ones for you? Seek advice from colleagues and friends, if you have contacts in recruitment agencies, ask them what you might need to progress in your industry. Make sure you know what your marketplace requires.

Academic v Experience

Academia is something which I have never found easy – I don't understand lots of theories and models. Professor Stephen Hawking will always be one of my heroes, but Quantum Physics... forget it!

I have always loved learning but learning in an academic environment has generally been a challenge. At school, my teachers never wrote on my report — "Could try harder". I always tried very hard, but just didn't get it unless it was very experiential learning linked with a really good experiment.

I will always remember studying Archimedes' Principle of Displacement. Our science teacher had encouraged us to shout "Eureka!" when we jumped into the bath that evening. I loved that the experiment was interactive — we all learnt from trying out it at home, although the school did receive a number of complaints the next day about flooded bathroom floors! If only all schooling was as interactive and experimental, then I am sure we would all learn more.

Since my school days, I have been very good at learning from experience and new situations, so there is hope for us all. I have always tried to maximise my own potential by constantly learning and have often 'punched above my weight' as the saying goes. However, if you are academically gifted and are also able to learn from your experiences, then how great you could be if you put them both together?

"You don't have to be great to get started, but you do have to get started to be great."

- Zig Ziglar

Upskilling or even Reskilling

Every year, look at your market and consider whether you need to upskill? What new technology, concepts, or ways of working are likely to impact your industry and business over the next few months or years? Is your business likely to outsource or enter into joint partnerships with other companies? Will your role still exist? If that is likely to happen in your business, then just moving to another company and waiting for the same thing to happen there perhaps isn't the best move. Do you need to look further ahead and reskill? Look out for the warning signs and don't get caught out!

Managing Your Self-development

Key questions to ask:

- What have you learnt about yourself recently?
- Do you prefer to stay within your comfort zone?
- When have you been outside your comfort zone recently? What did you learn about yourself?
- What opportunities do you have coming up that will encourage you to move outside your comfort zone?
- What personal qualities and attributes, do you need to develop, to improve or to progress in your career?
- What knowledge and skills do you need to develop?
- What new experiences do you feel a need to gain and how can you get that experience?

My Annual MOT

When you receive an email from your manager or HR inviting you to your Annual Appraisal or PDR (Personal Development Review), do you think (like most people): "Oh great, I really don't need that! I am so busy, do I really have to do this and talk about myself?"

However, stop and think for just a minute. Ask yourself: "Can I benefit from this?" The answer is YES — you just need to think differently and put some effort in.

Your company is giving you the opportunity to spend time thinking about you. Don't miss out on that opportunity. Even if your manager is useless at conducting appraisals, you can still create some value for yourself.

Look at the questions below and use your company's documentation to review your progress. Get a copy of your job description and measure yourself on what you are doing well and where you might need to develop. Additionally, source job descriptions of roles that you would like and create a plan to demonstrate to your manager that you have the capabilities to step up. Be honest with yourself and solicit feedback from people whom you trust and who will be honest with you.

Stop and reflect

This is your opportunity to reflect on what you have learnt and what you need to learn. Invest in your personal development and your future career opportunities:

- What do I want to do in the future?
- How employable am I?
- Would I want to work with me?

- Am I a good team player?
- What impact do I have on others?
- What feedback do I need to get from others?
- Do I network well and build contacts?
- Do I understand how my business works?
- Who could I get mentoring from?
- Who could I mentor?
- What great advice do I give other people that perhaps I should take more notice of?
- What extra responsibilities and opportunities could I take on at work?

Proactively manage your PDR and appraisal process. It's not an HR tick box exercise, it's about you, your career, your wellbeing and your future. You need to invest in it; you need to invest time in yourself in order to develop.

Chapter Three: Anticipating Change in your Working World

Life is about choices — develop yourself so you have the opportunity to make the right choices

Build awareness and take responsibility

As we all know, the working world is constantly changing. So, if you feel that your job or your working environment isn't changing, rest assured, it will do soon. So, don't get left behind.

I have always liked the phrase: "Being one step ahead of the game". This means that you should stop, reflect and anticipate on what you need to do to remain relevant and add value to your working world and environment. Try to think about what your job or business might look like in the short-term, say six months' time ...and the medium-term in three years' time...and the long-term in five years' time. Looking beyond five years might be a struggle, but you are the one who will benefit from the forward planning.

Raising your profile in your business or industry should be a natural part of your strategy to create future opportunities for yourself. However, first ask yourself whether you want to deal with 'you', whether you would want to work with 'you'? What do you have to offer other people? It's not all about taking; it's also about giving and the value you can give to others so that they will want to work and deal with you in the future. Understanding the impact you have on other people will influence both your self-awareness and any areas that you might need to develop.

Changing career is a huge challenge. You will have already built up the skills, knowledge, experience (and salary!) for your current job and career path, so to start all over again might seem like an impossible task. Making changes to your career in terms of a new direction and industry requires careful consideration — you don't suddenly want to end up in a worse situation if things suddenly go wrong.

Think about your own wellbeing. Think about potential changes to your career, over which you have no control, especially if you see risks on the horizon for your current career / job. For example, what might your current industry / profession look in the next few years? Now might be a good time to make a move to develop and protect yourself.

Wherever you are in your career, it's important to reflect on how many years will you realistically have to spend in your working environment before you can retire on the living standard you desire. So, you might as well make sure that you try to enjoy your career journey and to undertake occupations that give you a sense of pride, well-being and a self-worth.

For young adults coming into the working world, this might mean 50 years of planning your working career. Even if you are currently in your fifties, you could still have another twenty years to go before you can afford to retire. So, make the right choices and Future Proof Yourself to allow you to enjoy the journey.

Demonstrating the value that you can bring to your current role, or a new position, or a new company, isn't always easy. Looking for that new job can often feel like a full-time occupation in its own right, so it's time for you to be able to sell yourself and demonstrate the value that you can bring. This is why it's worth spending time thinking about your 'story'.

Ask yourself: where did you start? Why did you make certain key decisions in your career? What experiences and choices did you make along the way? What direction are you now wanting to go in and, most importantly, why should another organisation invest in you? What will the return on their investment be if they employ you?

Knowing your 'story' and the benefits you can bring to others is an important part of professionalism and will help you to Future Proof Yourself.

After all, if you don't do it for yourself, then who is going to do it for you?

Anticipating Change in your Working World

If only we all had a crystal ball. If only we knew what our business and industry would look like in the next few years, or even the next few months?

Networking and keeping up-to-date is essential to help anticipate change in your working world but be careful who you spend time with. Don't end up spending too much time with people who frequently start their sentences with:

- The trouble with this company/ industry is...
- I remember the time when...
- When I first started...
- Well, if they are not careful...

Instead talk to people who have great ideas, driving ambition, or different ways of thinking. You don't have to agree with them all the time, but they can generate good ideas for you to build upon.

Do you network outside of your company enough? Think about what you can you learn from other industries and how they do business.

Try to find a young mentor, somebody younger than you who thinks differently, a new generation with new enthusiasm. Talk to your clients informally to understand how they see the market, the industry, the environment, the world.

Whenever you have appraisals or one-to-one project reviews, have great questions ready for you and others to ponder:

- What changes do you see on the horizon in your working environment?

- What social trends may have an impact?
- What political, legal or economic trends may drive changes in your organisation?
- What technological developments may drive changes to your ways of working?

Disaster Companies

Whatever happened to?

- Kodak
- Yellow Pages
- HMV
- Blackberry
- Blockbuster
- Woolworths
- Toys R Us

These were all once great companies, but they didn't develop and keep pace with new technologies or new ways of working; they just carried on doing the same old thing and look at what happened to them. They are all really good examples of what 'not to do' in business. Now I know that you aren't a company per se, but as we have discussed earlier in this book, we all sell our time, knowledge, skills... etc, in return for a wage or a fee. In that sense we are all individual limited companies, no different to those 'Disaster Companies' listed above, just a lot smaller. So, don't let what happened to these companies happen to you!

Raising your profile – Personal Impact

Perception - how would you like to be perceived by others? How would you like people to describe you when you are not around?

Where do people get their perceptions of you from? The answer is in your behaviour. If you are not too keen on how people perceive you, then perhaps it's time to change some of your behaviours.

I often ask people to compare themselves against a famous brand. Which brand would best represent you and how you act and behave?

Give it some thought. If you chose a high-end brand, do you demonstrate the same quality and customer service in your everyday activities? If not, what could you do to change? What behaviours might you need to develop and improve?

At times people defend their behaviours by saying "But that's the way I am", which is a fair point; we don't want you to change your personalities, but we do have the ability to adapt and change our behaviours to suit different situations.

How professional are we? Do we do the right things in the right way and at the right time?

Raising your profile needs careful consideration. Here are a few questions to start you off:

Would you want to work with you? And why?

- If you have management responsibilities, would you want 'you' as a manager?
- What behaviours and attributes would you like others to see in you?

If you are trying to improve your profile internally with senior managers, you might like to think about:

- How do they make decisions?
- How do they think? And how can you learn to think like them?
- What do they look for in people they want to rely on?
- What types of people do they trust and listen to?
- What's their personality / behaviour style?
- How well do you answer their questions?
- How confident are you in front of them?
- Can you be one step ahead of them and pre-empt what they want?
- Operational v strategic - do you get the balance right when talking to them?

This is also applicable to key clients with whom you would like to improve your profile.

However, don't overdo it, don't be something you are not or somebody else.

Be 'you' with good self-awareness and responsibility which I think is a good starting point when trying to create your own style.

Other ways to improve your profile

- Be yourself and genuine.
- Build trust and two-way respect.
- Spend more time listening than talking.
- Use social media/ LinkedIn (but don't overdo it or people will think that is all you do all day).
- Network and build contacts.
- Develop expertise and be confident.
- Learn from others.
- Ask great questions of others.
- Don't try and be what you are not, or be like someone else.
- Watch and learn how others operate and work (people who you respect).
- Learn from their actions and behaviours.
- Do great work and be a great team member.
- Find positives in others and give positive feedback.
- Don't make it all about 'you'.
- Create the opportunity and time to talk with other people - show an interest in them.
- Ask yourself, "Who do I need to make a greater impact on in my working environment?"
- What influences these people and how do they make decisions?

"I don't like what you're telling me"

I once worked for a very prestigious organisation in the City of London. All sharp suits, polished shoes, silk ties and one's best cuff links!

I had spent the day coaching a rather challenging group of senior consultants who were not best pleased that they had been singled out for extra development by their Senior Partner (it was often seen as a weakness on their part rather than an opportunity to be given one-to-one coaching). At the end of my day's coaching I was, as usual, summoned to the Senior Partner's office to give my feedback on the day.

He began by asking: "What have you got for me?"

I explained my areas of concern with some of his team and the impact they were having on the business and other team members.

After I had finished my very honest and frank assessment, he looked at me sternly and said, "I don't like what you're telling me".

He got up from his chair and shut the door behind him. I sat silent, not wanting to justify my assessment any further, so he continued: "However, I respect the fact that you have got the bxxxxxx to come in here and tell me. So what should I do about it?"

You will earn more respect by being honest and sticking to your point. Learn to deliver feedback in an assertive manner and use silence to reinforce a point rather than waffling. Your profile will develop by you being 'you', whilst at the same time, appreciating how others work and communicate.

Developing your profile is about creating more choices and opportunities for yourself. If you don't do it, then who is going to do it for you?

Professional going to the theatre

Going to the theatre isn't cheap. However, it is worth it for a top West End professional production because you know it's going to be great. And you have decided to take your partner along or a good friend.

It's not just the cost of the show; it's the travel up to London, (which isn't cheap) but it will be worth it for a great professional production.

Then the meal beforehand and the drinks before the show (which aren't cheap) but will all be worth it for a great professional production (not to mention the cost of the ice cream!)

You're still in your seats as the show starts and the curtain goes up. You think it is going to be great — (it's not been cheap!) but for a professional West End Production it will be worth it.

The leading performers come on stage and start singing and dancing. You think, "This is going to be great", but then suddenly the cast suddenly stop, sigh and exclaim in unison: "Do you know how many times we've sung this damned song? We're fed up and want to go home."

You wouldn't be very happy, would you? It's not very professional, is it? I daresay you would complain vigorously and demand your money back.

Professional Responsibility

Do you act and behave in a professional manner at all times and perform to the best of your abilities? We expect it of other professional people, but do we practice professional responsibility?

The next time you go into work in the morning, think about what your body language is it saying to your colleagues. Are you being professional and showing that you are being present and there for your colleagues? Are you showing that you are ready and prepared for your day? Or, is your body language telling others that you don't want to be there? It's often an enlightening exercise to watch people walk into their working environments.

Think about other aspects of your work and how you deliver on what is expected of you. Professional responsibility relates to all of the areas covered in Future Proofing Yourself and means performing to the best of your abilities on an ongoing basis.

You expect other people to demonstrate professional responsibility when you use their services but do you demonstrate the same level of professionalism yourself in your everyday work? Can you have an off-day or, like that of the actors and actresses on the stage, you need to perform to the best of your potential at all times?

Career Changes

There will be times in your career when you sit and reflect and think that it's time for a change. It will be a tough decision which requires a lot of thought and a number of conversations with other people to seek their advice. Making the right decision is vital, financially, well-being and to continue your ability to Future Proof Yourself should be at the top of your list.

You may think; "What do I want to do? Well, I'm not really sure?"

It's a difficult question and it can be a tough situation if you are starting out in your career or looking to change. Trying to decide which way to go isn't easy.

It's often easier to start by listing the things you don't want to do, rather than what you do want to do. Get rid of some of your thoughts of what you wouldn't want to do and then start to narrow down to the things you would like to do.

There are a great number of tests on the internet to help you decide what sort of job or career might be best for you.

Do you feel fulfilled in your current position? If not, what would make you feel more fulfilled?

As we said earlier in the book, the difficulty is not just in working out what you think you **do want** to do, but also in realising what you really **don't want** to do in your career.

So, some simple questions:

What don't I want to do?

Ask yourself:

- What environments wouldn't I enjoy?
- What types of work wouldn't I want to do?
- Would I prefer lots of interaction or minimal interaction?
- Would I rather work in a team or on my own?
- What would bore me?
- What would I hate to have to get up every morning to do?
- How far and how much time would I be prepared to commute?

So now on to thinking about what it is that you **do** want to do. Remember that your thought processes can often change during your life and career as your passions and desires change.

What do I want to do?

- What am I good at?
- What do I enjoy?
- What's my passion?
- What am I willing to work hard at?
- What can I get paid for?
- Where does my work-life balance fit in?

Talk to people who you know well:

- What do they like / don't like about their jobs?
- What sounds interesting or doesn't sound interesting?
- Are you best working in a team or on my own?
- Would you prefer a big corporate or a small organisation?
- Realistically describe your ideal job/career.
- Why is this your ideal job / career and what unique skills / passions have you got which could make this happen?
- What interests you/ where do you feel 'in flow'?
- Who could you talk to about their jobs and careers to get ideas?
- Do you consider career progression as upwards move or a sideways / lateral move?
- What lateral move may be of interest?
- Does fear of the unknown hold you back?

- If 'yes' what are you afraid might happen?
- How likely is this to happen?
- What could you do to avoid this / be prepared for this?

Do I just want a job?

Focus on your work-life balance. For many people, it's not just about work and building a career — you might not want to chase a career, to play corporate games or to change the world. However, remember that you have to keep yourself employable for the next 'however many' years. Will you still have the right skills to be employable in your line of work? What experience, qualifications and marketable skills might you need to stay current and of value to the companies out there?

This can be a bit scary for some people who enjoy and are motivated by staying inside their current comfort zones. But reality is reality and we all need to learn and embrace the need to develop and change within our environments.

Welcome to the next 50 years of your life

How will you keep yourself employable for the rest of your career?

"Welcome to the next 50 years of your life — how are you going to keep yourself employable for this length of time?"

Perhaps not the best introduction to a group of young adults starting their first day at work on their apprenticeship programme. But the reality is, that going forward we will all have to work longer and longer. It doesn't matter how old we are or where we are in our career. It's a question we all need to think about when we are thinking of our career and how we are going to fund our retirement.

A few Tips for the Younger Generation

The harsh reality of life is that if you have just finished your education, the chances are that you might have to stay in the working environment for another 50 years. Yes, this can be a very disturbing thought.

For many young adults, there is the social pressure to build a career quickly and earn good money. This is often easier said than done. Knowing what you want to do is often the biggest challenge. Very few people leave their education knowing exactly what they want to do. So what is the best way to get started?

You can't expect to walk straight out of your education into a dream job, so it will take time and patience.

Keep Learning

This doesn't mean that you have to go out and pass more exams, although this does naturally help.

However, much learning comes from your experiences. Learn what you like to do and what you don't like to do, learn from friends and people you were in education with. What are they doing for work, does that interest you? Talk to family and family friends of any age group and show interest in what they do; if it's of interest, could you do some work experience at their place of work? If you don't ask you will never know.

Whatever job you do, keep learning from your experiences and doing new jobs and tasks. The more people to whom you talk, the more you will learn.

How does it all work?

So you get your first job; it's a relief to you (and often even more so to your parents!) that you are now up and running. Naturally the first thing to do is to be enthusiastic and learn your job inside out, to be good at what you do so people want to keep employing you. Remember, you are there to help the business and add value. The business isn't there for you.

Whatever job you do, learn how the business works, who does what and how the business makes money and operates. Learning how a business works is so important because where ever you work in your career, you will need to learn how the commercials work, even if you work in the public sector or for charities.

What are your passions?

Thinking about a job and career for the rest of your life is a daunting prospect. Wouldn't it be good to work doing something for which you have a real passion and which you really enjoy? So why not? I think it's safe to say in today's environment that you can make money and build a career and a job doing almost anything, as long as people are willing to pay for the end service or the product.

Type in a subject of your choice into the internet and you will find an organisation who will supply you with the service or product. Anything is possible.

Setting up a photography business or art online couldn't be easier. Creating a marketing business or buying and selling a product are all possibilities as long as you learn how to do it and understand how to make it viable. Above all, if you want to make something work for you, you will have to work hard and be committed.

So, what are you good at? What do you find interesting? What would you enjoy doing even if you didn't get paid for doing it?

Go and research ideas; you have the internet at your fingertips. Look at what companies do. Don't spend all your time looking at recruitment sites. These sites can generate ideas, but go a step further and look at companies that do things which you are interested in. Try to talk to people in similar companies and get a foot in the door.

As we said earlier, securing your first paid job is a relief all round. Be careful not to take it for granted; this is the start of your story which people will be interested in when you apply for future jobs.

During your first job, learn as much as you can. As we have already mentioned before, try to move only if it's to better yourself or for a good reason. In a few years' time you will want your CV to look good so people can see you have thought about your career progression, and that you haven't just moved for money or because you have fallen out with people.

Create a story of progression with good reasons as to why you have moved. Demonstrate how you have performed along with what you have learnt along the way. Developing a good work experience story will impress future employers.

We are a Limited Company

We are all limited companies. We sell our time, skills, knowledge, experience and untold amounts of passion and enthusiasm to our company. In exchange we receive a wage and hopefully a few other perks and benefits. But how will you continue to represent a good investment for your company? Should your company employ you or a new piece of equipment — which will offer the better return on investment? That's the harsh reality of no more 'jobs for life'.

This is why your Annual Reviews are so important and why, if anything, we should do reviews more frequently. Remember don't wait for your managers to run them for you. Ask them and remind them repeatedly.

Think about what you want to achieve in your career

Which way is your industry going? Does it play to your strengths and passions? What skills are suitable? What skills, knowledge or experiences might you need to develop? How marketable are your strengths? What skills might you need to acquire and develop to become a more valuable proposition to yourself and future employers?

Acquire those skills and make learning a part of your day-to-day activities.

When you move jobs, always try to do so under your terms so that you can remain in control. Be careful about making rash decisions such as leaving a job following a small disagreement or because you felt undervalued at the time. Be aware that moving jobs for short-term opportunities such as a potential pay rise usually represents a short-term sticking plaster.

Try to focus upon your aspirations for your career and make any job move for the right reasons; ones that put you, your CV and your career story in a good light. Use your network or your mentor for advice. Talk to your boss as much as possible about your career and any opportunities on the horizon, try and be open and as honest as you can.

Always try to leave your job on good terms, with your reputation and integrity intact. In most industries, everybody seems to know everybody else, and you will no doubt come into contact with old colleagues again in your career, either as future colleagues or even clients. Word spreads quickly if you leave on bad terms and, the chances are, it will cause you problems in the future.

Always try and make career moves for the right reasons: to gain new experiences, new skills, greater responsibility or for the opportunity to gain more success.

Keep your CV up-to-date and record your achievements and successes. Do this when you have your appraisals and PDR reviews. Take time to review your skills, attributes and experiences and what direction you are going in so you can make the right choices. This can help to keep you motivated and fresh in the knowledge that you are developing and moving forwards with your career. Plus, if a new opportunity comes along unexpectedly, you are prepared. Know your CV and know your career story.

Stop relying upon your CV — focus on your knowledge, skills and experience.

At a certain point in our careers, our age will become an issue and our CV won't always help us to get back in front of potential employers, especially if we need to go through the recruitment consultant process from the outset. By listing our jobs and dates of employment, we can't hide our career story, especially if we might have had a tough time of it in recent years.

We can all pick up bad habits, become too expensive, or a little too set in our ways. Perhaps 'we' are not what our companies want for the next few years in terms of team members or managers to drive the business forward.

If your work and your career aren't at the forefront of your mind like they used to be and perhaps your energy levels aren't as high anymore, then frustration can creep in . We don't secure the interviews anymore, let alone the jobs. People ask for our CVs and promise to get in contact, but when they don't, we start to feel that we are being left behind.

So how do we buck the system and show the true value of what can we do without people judging us based solely upon our CV? We need to create a different way of promoting ourselves and working for our future. Working freelance can sometimes be a better option — this allows you to create marketing material, social media profiles and blog posts to engage with potential customers instead of concentrating solely on engaging with potential employers. The rules nowadays are different and don't involve CVs that fail to paint you in a good light:

- Your LinkedIn profile can have testimonials and achievements to engage with potential new customers.
- You can write articles and posts to demonstrate your ideas and thoughts.
- Facebook pages can generate new ideas and creativity.
- Instagram can inspire people with visual thoughts.
- Twitter can help create a presence and profile to demonstrate your knowledge skills and experience.

All these different approaches can make you attractive to people looking to hire your skills without the need for a CV.

The rules are constantly changing and we need to learn to play a new game to keep ourselves relevant and of value to our new customers. It's a big shift in mindset, but the opportunities are endless.

Should I stay or should I go?

Be mindful of staying in a job too long, but at the same time, don't move jobs simply for the sake of it. If you love what you are doing, the culture of your organisation, or your existing work:life balance, then the grass isn't always greener elsewhere. Always think about the longer-term consequences.

If your vision is for a senior position, you need to strike the right balance between moving too quickly (and not demonstrating any loyalty or good decision-making) versus staying too long (and having your ambition and desire called into question).

It is time to move on internally or externally when:

- You are getting bored or the excitement has gone from your job.
- You are not acquiring any new experience or developing any new skills or knowledge.
- The job is too easy — you are in a comfort zone and starting to go stale.
- You crave new challenges or opportunities.
- You stop looking forward to going to work.

Build your career for the right reasons (as discussed) and review your current job and future career aspirations on a regular basis. Collect experiences, attributes, achievements and successes rather than just a series of jobs.

Future Proof Yourself and take control. Ask yourself what the next step should be in developing your career?

Remember - you don't have to be great to get started, but you do have to get started to be great. It doesn't matter what your definition of 'great' might be — mine is to be happy.

Professional Qualifications

There are many careers and professions which demand the correct qualifications and require you to be able to demonstrate competence and expertise in your field of work.

What qualifications does your industry, career, or business require you to have? Do your research — it is all at your fingertips. Talk to people in your network for advice or contact the relevant associations and institutes.

Could a lack of qualifications in the early part of your career represent a potential blockage further down the line, leaving you unable to Future Proof Yourself?

Knowing in advance and making the right decisions and choices is essential.

Research and get advice now and plan out how are you going to manage it.

It's a tough option to work and study at the same time, but it's normally the best (and only) route for many. Invest in your time and get yourself very well organised between work:study:life.

Try to put your studying high up on your Priority List and give it the time and focus it merits. Make sure your family and friends know how important it is to you and ask for their support and understanding. No one can do it for you, and you will be the one to benefit.

Dealing with recruitment consultants

"So, I told them what I thought and what they needed to be doing... they've got it all wrong... they don't understand the industry..." "Maybe, or maybe not", I thought as my friend continued his rant. "They need to look at my experience and skillset and realise the value that I can bring to businesses... I don't need to be told by some spotty kid what the industry is doing." I remained silent but thought to myself: "It's their game and their rules though... ranting at them is not going to help you get in front of a perspective employer — you need to learn to play their game." My friend never did secure another job through that agency; he annoyed them too much before the process had ever got started.

It can be very frustrating being reliant on recruitment consultants. Naturally, recruitment consultants vary greatly, but as with any networking, build relationships — they are only trying to do their job, often in tough circumstances.

In your career, try to build relationships with people who are recruitment consultants. (Naturally, if you are in a management position, this can be easier when you deal with them when you are recruiting.)

If you are in a management position, you will no doubt come into contact with them frequently whilst recruiting — the rest of us use LinkedIn! So, make a call and have a chat to find out what's happening in your market. Try to do this when you are not looking for a job — you will gain important information on the market / industry requirements and be able to make career choices based upon this information.

Have some good pre-prepared questions to ask them and try and provide them with some useful contacts in exchange for their information. Remember, it's their business and it's how they make money.

You will probably not be the most important person they speak to (even though you might think you are) — think how you can help them so that they can help you. Match their enthusiasm and energy, listen, ask great question, put the effort in to manage the relationship, be proactive and honest.

Try to build a partnership and relationship with recruitment consultants. To not be in control of your own recruitment process can be frustrating, especially if you have been fully in control of your job and career to date. However, looking for a job in today's world can often be a full-time job in itself, so invest in the relationship and spend your time preparing and researching.

What's your Story?

Applying for jobs and engaging with prospective employers is a tough gig in today's world, the competition is tough out there.

One thing that will help you to stand out is by preparing your 'story'.

Try to position your CV so that it has purpose and relevance for the positions you have held and the changes and choices that you have made. Make sure you consider carefully how you present yourself and the value you can bring to new employers.

Link your job roles together so there is a flow and logic behind why you have made those changes in your career. This gives interviewers the confidence that you represent a good investment and have control over your career, rather than having bounced out of one job and into another purely for the sake of it.

If you are new to the working world, create a story for yourself through the responsibilities you might have held whilst in education and link these with any job experience you might have had.

An HR manager in Heaven

An esteemed HR manager unfortunately died and was sent up to Heaven in a lift (even God has automated the way he works these days!). After a long lift ride, the doors opened and the HR manager walked out and over to the pearly gates of Heaven where he meets St Peter.

The HR manager approached St Peter and said: "Hello, I am an esteemed HR Manager and I have come to join you in Heaven." St Peter nodded and replied, "Yes I have been expecting you."

"Well can I come in then?", the HR manager continued.

St Peter looked the HR manager up and down and said, "Well, it's not as simple nor as easy as that. First of all, you need to take the lift down to Hell and spend a day there. Then, you can come back up to Heaven and spend a day here with us. After that, I will then ask you to decide where you want to spend your eternal days."

The HR manager gets into the lift, presses the button, and is taken down to Hell.

When he arrives, he is pleasantly surprised to see that Hell is a colourful place with flowers and gardens. People approach the HR manager and welcome him to their world. The HR Manger gets taken out for lunch where there is laughter and fun and a real sense of wellbeing.

At the end of the day, the HR manager reluctantly gets back into the lift and goes back up to Heaven. He would have happily stayed in the warm and welcoming place called Hell.

The HR manager then spends his second day in Heaven on a cloud, feeding white doves and plucking a harp. Frankly it is all very boring and mundane.

After that, he goes back to see St Peter. The HR manager informs him told him that he would like to spend his eternal days in Hell. St Peter reluctantly agrees to his irreversible decision and the HR manager gets back into the lift and descends to Hell.

When he arrives, he is shocked to see that Hell is now dark and dingy with grey skies and devoid of any colour. Everybody now ignores the HR manager as they walk by, looking down and drawn of any happiness.

The HR manager heads straight away to see the devil, realising the ramifications of his decision, and insists upon knowing why there was such a big difference between now and his experience two days ago.

The Devil laughed: "You're the HR manager — surely you must have realised that back then we were recruiting?"

The moral of the story is to do your research before joining a new company. Make sure it's a good fit for you and your career aspirations and can help you to develop the lifestyle that you desire.

Chapter Four: Managing Your Key Skill Sets

What do you need to do to keep ahead of the game?

Be a great version of yourself, maximise your potential and your opportunities.

As stated previously, we are all limited companies. We sell our time, expertise, skills, knowledge, experience and bundles of energy and enthusiasm. And, in return, we hopefully receive a salary and various benefits. Like any other company which wants to stay relevant and to survive, we also need to upskill and provide great value for our products or services.

So, how do we manage this, or does it just pass us by as we plod through our careers hoping for the best? Do we just focus on the tasks and activities in front to of us or do we try to look ahead? Being ahead of the game and in control doesn't just happen — it takes time and effort. What's your strategy to stay ahead of the game and relevant in your working environment?

A good place to start this process is with your networking. Who is in your network and does it need managing? We all need help in one way or another, so who can you help and who can help you? My network includes a lot of people who think differently to me. This is great, as I know how I think and perceive situations, so it's great to get another perspective or viewpoint and understand how other people see the same situations. A good network is an extension of your own skills, knowledge and experience which you can tap into whenever required. So invest in networking and help others whenever you can – you will reap the benefits.

As we have said before, developing your skills is vital to being able to Future Proof Yourself. However, it's not just your technical skills that need constantly updating, it's also vital that you keep your social and communication skills up-to-date. You may be technically gifted, but often the challenge lies in getting your message across so that others can buy in to your ideas and concepts. Learn to influence others and negotiate well.

Being able to promote yourself and your ideas will help key decision makers to utilise your key attributes. Therefore, we need to learn how to think like key decision makers (our own senior managers or clients) and how they make decisions, in order to influence them. Being able to access their level of thinking is vital so we can understand their decision-making processes — this allows us to fit in and become a person of influence.

Most good influencers are excellent at understanding situations by asking great questions and being inquisitive as to what is around them. If you have an excellent understanding of a particular situation or problem, you are in a much better position to come up with the best solution.

Being technically proficient is often only half the battle. Although we must always be developing our technical skills to remain professionally competent, keeping our communication skills sharp requires almost as much attention. This allows us to communicate with all levels of authority and to present our ideas and ourselves more effectively so that people can say "Yes" more often.

Make situations happen. Don't be the person who sits and waits to get involved. Talk to as many people as possible, generate well thought-out ideas, be a good leader of yourself and make your ideas happen.

Technology is a key part of our working world, so how does it all work? What will you need to know and learn? How can it help you in your career? What will big business and industry be using in the next few years and are you on board with it? These questions, along with plenty more, need to be addressed on a regular basis.

After all, if you don't do it for yourself, then who is going to do it for you?

Networking skills

Networking isn't just about going to a networking event with lots of business cards and introducing yourself along the lines of: "Hello, my name's David and I run great training courses. So, what do you do?"... and then expect to win lots of business!

Networking is about getting to really know people, how you can help them and how they can help you, in order to create a mutually beneficial relationship.

What can you learn from other people? They might be in a different business or industry to you, so ask yourself what are their challenges, how do they work, and what are their thoughts, ideas or experiences? All this free learning is right there in front of you, so make sure you don't miss out on it.

It's important to network well with people in your business, but do you know how your business really works? Most of us work in silos, concentrating solely on our own areas of expertise, so we need to get out there and talk to people, we need to have great questions to ask them. We can obtain all this free learning from our networks.

I think the golden rule of networking should be as follows: *"I know what I think and what I do, but in order to learn more, I need to go and find out what others think and what others do."* This mindset will create more opportunities and you will learn more.

Listening effectively is a great way to make a positive impact when you meet somebody for the first time. If you can show that you are really interested in them by asking intelligent questions and listening well you can then ask more relevant questions so you can get to know and understand that person quickly. You get to find out about them and how you could potentially help them or benefit from knowing them. People like to be listened to and will see you as a positive influence by doing more listening than talking. Naturally you need to talk but talk about topics that are of interest to the other person rather than just trying to sell yourself.

I once nearly took up smoking because a colleague of mine smoked and always seemed to know more about what was going on in the business than the rest of the team. His career progressed faster than ours as opportunities and good projects always seemed to come his way. He used to sit at his desk facing the corridor where the senior managers had their offices, his cigarettes and lighter always ready for action next to his computer. He would wait for certain senior managers to come out of their office to go for a cigarette, and then quickly follow them. He was a fabulous networker and got into lots of great informal conversations with senior managers which generated ideas and opportunities. Now I am not encouraging people to take up smoking, but it does make you think —networking certainly worked for him.

When networking externally, try to get others to talk as this is all free information: how do they do things and generate ideas? People often like to boast about what they do and in doing so, will give you too much information.

Networking opportunities

- Who do you need to know better in your business? (people to connect with / business partners).
- When networking, what can you do for them?
- Who do you need to build a relationship with outside your business and why?
- Who can help you in your career: friends and family, a work mentor?

- Who would be good to keep in contact with — old colleagues, friends from school / education / university?
- How frequently do you purposefully spend time networking to expand your exposure in your working world? Would you benefit from increasing this time? What opportunities are available to you?
- Who inspires you?
- Who helps you to think differently and why?
- What helps you to think differently and why?
- Where helps you to think differently and why?

Networking on social media is a great way of keeping in contact and up-to-date with what people are doing. Add your comment of support but don't try and hijack posts (this often happens) — remember, it's not all about you.

Being well-read will allow you to have a balanced input into conversations, but don't unduly exaggerate your knowledge, otherwise you can get quickly caught out and look very stupid very quickly. Don't compete and try to outdo your new contact. Don't get into heated debates; instead, let the other party have their say and move on — at least you will have made them feel good about themselves, which could ultimately work in your favour.

Build contacts by sending your contacts posts or articles that are of interest and are relevant or of value to them. When you hear about an industry event or a good networking opportunity that's worth attending, pass the information on to interested contacts, and let them know why you thought it might benefit them.

Take opportunities to speak at conferences and other networking events

Public speaking is a great opportunity to put yourself out there and build your network and contacts whilst developing your profile and brand. When you get the opportunity, plan, practice, and obtain feedback before you deliver. This will raise your profile so people can see you as an authority in your field.

LinkedIn

LinkedIn can act as your online CV / PR campaign, but don't overdo it. Create a profile and ask for feedback from people in your network. Try to create visuals and make it interesting. Be honest and collect genuine testimonials but don't oversell yourself. Be positive and look at your profile through the readers' eyes. Ask yourself how you want them to view you after reading your profile?

Be factual and honest (it can be a small world in some industries!) and if you are job hunting, know what's in your profile so you can answer any questions assuming the interviewer has done his/her research.

Always write a personal invite when connecting with other people and accept requests to connect with a personal "Thank you".

As previously noted, don't hijack other peoples' posts and be careful not to over-promote yourself when writing your posts.

LinkedIn is a great way for keeping in touch when people move on to new jobs, so take the time to add personal comments such as, "Congrats on your new job", but don't just rely upon LinkedIn – a personal phone call is better if they are a very good contact.

Strategic thinking

Developing your career in life means changing your thinking in order to progress upwards.

If you come from a team member role or are new to management, it can be a challenge not to just stay in an operational mindset which is all about getting tasks done and completing processes. We can spend far too much time with colleagues having the conversation: "What this company needs to do is...", and so on.

Learn to change your thinking from a short-term mindset (concerned with tasks and processes) towards a longer-term mindset of strategic thinking (strategy and visionary). If it was your business, your money and your responsibility, what would you do? Having to think about future plans, sales and market opportunities isn't that easy — what to make and what to buy, too little or too much either way can cause huge problems in the event of a change in the markets Try to think about company decisions as if you had put your name to them. When you work for yourself as self-employed or a freelancer, it's a totally different way of thinking to a salaried job — there is nowhere to hide.

You need to develop exposure to this strategic way of thinking and how to remain one step ahead of the competition in cut-throat environments.

It can be easy to be a campaigner or a complainer and point out whatever's wrong to whoever is prepared to listen. However, it's a lot tougher to be a decision-maker and to take responsibility. Any politician who is not in government finds it easy to complain and moan about everything, but if they do happen to get into government, they soon realise that it isn't as easy as previously thought.

Read good articles on entrepreneurs who have risked everything for their business. How did they make it happen and what's their way of thinking? How do they see the future and how do they proactively deal with change?

Try to ask more questions from respected senior managers and directors on why your business does certain things and has certain ways of working. Show you are genuinely interested and care about the business and its future — you will get a much better response than being critical.

Most importantly, understand the finances and how it all works at the next level up.

Learn to think like entrepreneurs and senior directors; expose yourself to conversations with them to understand how they see things and make decisions.

Strategic thinking is vital for your development. Look beyond your everyday tasks, your job, your team and learn to think and understand how the whole business works as a whole. This is something rarely covered in appraisals, development plans or learning objectives, but you need to make sure it's now covered in yours.

Go and make it happen for you.

Influencing and communicating at all levels

Understanding others

The Church

A group exercise on 'Understanding Others' which I've carried out successfully in the past, goes like this: draw a picture of a church on a flip chart in front of a group of people and ask them what 'Church' means to them?

Depending how diverse the group is, you will receive differing comments about love, peace, togetherness, and probably a lot more besides! What this exercise helps to demonstrate is that we can see the same concept from many different perspectives. To help understand other people, having the ability to ask and understand why somebody thinks in a certain way is vitally important.

I then ask the group: "If I was going to influence you with my views of the church, what would I need to do?"

The reply usually starts off along the lines of having a strong message, being believable, or being passionate. The group then begins to realise that I would need to understand their views first and understand **why** they hold those views and opinions.

This demonstrates how important it is to understand other people's views first. However, how often do we try to convince, influence and communicate with people by just expressing our views without trying to understand theirs?

Being a good communicator isn't just about getting your message across; it's about listening and, more importantly, understanding why someone thinks in a particular way. What are their views, what are their feelings and what are their beliefs based upon? Once you are aware of all this, you can decide how best to influence that person by talking about the topics that are important and of interest to them.

Understand others first before trying to make yourself understood.

Having excellent consultancy skills is very important in making the right impact on other people.

To be a great consultant, first you need information, particularly information on the person or business you are dealing with. You can't make recommendations and proposals unless you understand their needs, wants and desires. It is important that you personalise your communication rather than just throwing a lot of mud at the wall.

Often salespeople will make the mistake of trying to sell to people instead of helping people to buy from them. This is done by first understanding the other person's needs, wants, and desires, before making the most appropriate recommendation based upon the information gained.

Audi Story - Audi TT

I have never really been into cars.

However, one day my family decided we should go to the local Audi dealership to look for a new car for me. It was a wet Sunday afternoon and not much else happening, so I reluctantly agreed. We turned up at the dealership, and as we entered the showroom, there was a gleaming, sexy-looking Audi TT which was very pleasing on the eye.

My son said, "We are getting that one Dad!"

My daughter added, "If you get that car, you can start picking me up from school."

And my wife just said, "Mmmmmmm."

We stood admiring the car for a while before a very bright and enthusiastic sales person came over and we got talking. The salesperson asked, “Do you like the car? Would you like to take it for a test drive?”, to which I replied, “Yes please!”

Before long, we were out on the open road. My children convinced me there was plenty of room in the back, but my wife just sat there and said, “Mmmmmm.”

We were out for a while and really put the car through its paces. I must admit, I felt slightly guilty because when we returned to the dealership, as the car was rather dirty due to the weather and muddy roads. The salesperson greeted us enthusiastically and enquired whether we liked the car. I confirmed that we all loved it. “Excellent”, replied the salesperson, “Let’s sit down and go through some figures.”

“Buy it?”‘ I queried, “ I’m not buying it, why would I buy an Audi TT?” I’m 6”1’ — I could get into that car, but I would struggle to get out of it! I needed a car that did 55mpg as I drive 25,000 miles a year... where would I put my golf clubs and bike... plus what about weekends away?

Sorry, I might have desired an Audi TT along with the rest of my family, but what I actually needed was a boring fuel-efficient estate. The salesperson then became cross and blamed me for wasting his time, but at no point did the salesperson establish my needs, wants and desires. If you want to influence and persuade somebody, you need to first spend time understanding how they see things and what are their needs, wants, and desires.

In the salespersons’ case, they could have asked:

- What did I currently drive and why did I choose that car?
- What did I need my new car for?

- Information about my lifestyle and whether I used the car for work?

Nelson Mandela

Bill Clinton once said of Nelson Mandela: "95% of the time we disagreed, but I'm sure that 100% of the time, he understood why I thought that way."

How often do we spend our time trying to get our point across, instead of understanding how the other person might see things? And, just as importantly, why might they think that way?

If we understand how others see things first, it makes it easier to work to a consensus, since we can come up with ideas that suit both parties. Naturally, that requires patience and high tolerance levels... but that's a story for another day.

Would you want to work with 'you'?

What are you like as a team player? Would you want to work with 'you' and have 'you' on your team? Do you have the patience and understanding to work well with others, do you give other people time, do you listen to them?

There is hardly a role in today's business environment that doesn't involve working with other people in some way.

Focus on understanding how your colleagues and other team members prefer to work, how they like to communicate and they like to receive their information. What motivates them? You're not their manager but you will, I expect, collaborate with them or ask them for favours from time to time. If so, think about the impact you have on others so they are happy to help you and work with you.

Be honest with others (when you need their help) and look to help them (but don't overdo it).

Acknowledge their efforts and hard work and give honest and positive feedback.

Be compassionate to others, look for their strengths and positives in them as a person. We can all strive to do more of this, to try and be more tolerant and patient of others. As a consequence, people will like working for you more. How do we know this? Well, most of us appreciate it when others show a genuine interest in us.

Treat your boss like a client

Many people complain about their bosses and feel that they are not understood by them. I have run hundreds of management programmes and can certainly understand why managers and their team members often view work and business from very different perspectives.

I have written (what I consider!) a wonderful course called 'How to Manage your Manager' but I have only ever run it twice. Why? Because the managers are not keen to pay for it, even though they should, as the key message is to treat your manager like a client.

Understand what is important to your boss or manager:

- How do they like information presented to them?
- What is their working style?
- How do they make decisions?
- Do they like to talk about out of work subjects and be sociable?
- Or is it all about work?

- Do they have any hidden agendas?
- What are the politics like within the company?
- What influences their decision-making process?
- Are they career-based or company-focused?
- What critical time factors do they face in making decisions?
- What specific pressures they are under?

Do great work for them and get to know their standards and how they want you to work? Use this to pre-empt what they might need before they ask you for it.

Yes, as managers, they should proactively communicate with their team members on all the points above. However, that doesn't always happen, so don't just complain about them, take the lead and 'manage your manager' by asking great questions.

Assertive Communication

Assertiveness is about having the ability to say the right things, in the right way and at the right time. And, in doing so, making it much more likely that you will get what you want and the other person will be happy with that.

However, how often do we say the wrong thing, in the wrong way, at the wrong time? Sometimes this might be deliberate, to wind somebody up. Along with sarcasm, it's an aggressive form of communication; we might feel better for saying it and enjoy the joke, but often the other person isn't thinking the same thing, feeling like it's a bit of a put-down.

Being assertive is about deciding what you want and being clear about asking for it. If you don't ask you don't get. What is the worst thing someone can say in response? No?

And, if they do say 'No', you can always ask 'Why?' Try to discuss and understand why the other person thinks that way and how they have arrived at that decision. Knowing this information will put you in a much better position than not knowing it. You will now know what you need to do in the future to convince and influence that person.

Making an impact through your career

When you are young and new to the working environment, don't act as if you don't know anything and are waiting to be told what to do. Be smart, show your competence, step up, show good self-awareness, take responsibility and do whatever you do in a confident manner in order to reach your potential. Likewise, if you are a more mature worker, don't act like it and tell everybody that you have been there, done that and got the t-shirt. Show energy, enthusiasm, a keen sense of being part of a team, and demonstrate how keen you are to still learn and grow.

Patience and Tolerance

A lot of what we cover in this book might seem obvious and you could think, "Yes, but I know that already." However, how do you demonstrate these skills and behaviours? Do you have the patience and tolerance to deal with all your family, friends, colleagues and clients?

As my wife would say: "When you get frustrated with somebody, just humor them." It's a good tip.

Demonstrate patience, tolerance and a measure of humility — this will help you to become a person of real influence with whom people will always want to deal.

Personality Profiles – Behavioural Styles

I expect that at some stage in your career you will have completed a Personality Profile or a Behavioural Styles Psychometric Test.

If so, try to find wherever you have filed it away, either in a drawer or a computer file. Take a moment to study it again. So far in this book, we have looked at how people see things from a different perspective, and how they are motivated by different values. It's now time to look at how people have different preferred styles of communicating and receiving information.

Understanding these preferences will make your life a lot easier — you will be to choose the right communication style for all the people you come into contact in your working life.

Do they want a style which is:

- Detailed with facts and figures?
- Straight to-the-point with no waffle?
- Building a relationship of understanding and trust? or;
- Faster-moving action with feel-good factor and benefits?

We all communicate in different ways. There isn't a 'right' or a 'wrong' way of communicating. Don't think of other people as 'difficult', think of them as having different preferred styles of communication or ways of working.

People may see you as having a different style to them, but you're not difficult, are you?!

Learn to use these profiles and reports to fully understand your preferred communication or working style. Understand how you communicate or deal with certain situations. Take time to observe other people and their preferred styles so that you can communicate more effectively by adapting your style accordingly.

I have often been asked, "Why is it me that has to adapt and change my prepared style?"

And my answer is... you can't control other people, but you can control your own responses and behaviours. For example, if you are dealing with a person who prefers detailed facts and figures, by communicating in a manner that supplies them with the right information in the right format, you will be able to communicate more effectively and easily.

If you would like better relationships with a wider range of people and want to be able to communicate effectively, learn to adapt your style with the people you work with. It does make life a lot easier.

I once consulted for a firm of stockbrokers in the city of London. After undertaking some behavioural profiling on the brokers, I then asked them to try to profile their clients according to their preferred communication style. At the end of the process, we found that most brokers could only sell and deal with clients possessing certain behavioural styles. Normally ones similar to themselves.

We then practised Awareness Training of the different communication styles and how the brokers could adapt their delivery in order to communicate more effectively with a wider range of clients. It was a great success, and life became far easier for the brokers as they could now deal with a wider range of clients.

Being able to understand your own communication style in order to communicate effectively by understanding others and their styles and motivations is essential in building better business and working relationships.

Remember, there should be no such thing as a difficult person; it's just somebody with whom we haven't yet learnt how to effectively communicate. This is a really good exercise to practise with some of your family and friends... but perhaps that's a different story or a different book for another day?

Getting on other people's levels

I was invited to spend a day with the Managing Director (MD) of a consultancy business and his group of directors, to see if I could help them improve their internal communication, develop key strategies and create a clear vision for the business.

I spent some time with the directors, both individually and as a group, to understand their thoughts and feelings on what future development might be required.

The day went very well and by the end of it, I felt that I had a clear understanding of what the group of directors needed to help them all develop and improve as a Senior Leadership Team. At the close, I sat down with the MD and HR Director to explain my findings to them and what I thought the next steps needed to be. They seemed very onboard with my ideas, so much so I went for my close: "So, based on everything that we've discussed and talked about, shall we put a date in the diary to kickstart the development work?"

The MD (Andrew) smiled at me and said: "Not so fast... I'd like you to write me a detailed proposal first." Now Andrew's style was straight-to-the-point, big picture, without a huge amount of detail — he preferred visual explanations with diagrams and pictures.

We shook hands and I promised that he would have his proposal in the next few days. The HR Director (Anita) accompanied me back to the reception area so I took the opportunity to ask her, "Anita, Andrew doesn't really want a detailed written proposal, does he?"

"No he doesn't", she replied, "just give him a colourful PowerPoint proposal with lots of visuals and graphs."

So, I went home and gave it to my son (who was 17 years old at the time) and who was great with PowerPoint. We won the business (and I never did give my son any commission).

Working out how other people want to receive their information and how they like to communicate will help you get on with more people and will help to make life a lot easier for you.

Presenting yourself – Selling yourself – The value you bring

"So what do you do?" "I run Management Development training courses and Personal Effectiveness courses, along with one-to-one coaching sessions and talks at conferences."

Or in a nut shell, "I help clever people to maximise their potential by helping them to Future Proof themselves."

Which reply is likely to increase more conversation and interest? How would you reply? Don't tell people **what** you do, tell them **the value** that you bring.

Brand 'you'

Earlier on in the book, you were asked how you would like to be perceived by others and what famous brand might represent you best.

On my training courses and seminars, I often ask who, with only 5 minutes preparation, would be prepared to come to the front of the group and present the value they bring to their organisation, clients and team members. There are usually very few people who are willing to take me up on that offer!

For some reason, we don't like talking about ourselves, let alone presenting the benefits and the value we bring to our working environment. This is all wrong. We should be comfortable and competent in presenting ourselves and demonstrating factually the value we are able to bring.

If you can't wave your flag who is going to do it for you? It is called professionalism; top sports people, actors, performers and singers know why they are successful, what their fans want, and how to deliver what they want.

So why shouldn't we? If you are customer-facing, you (like me) will no doubt often get asked: "What can you do for us?". If you can't instantly articulate the value you can bring to your clients or customers, you will instantly lose credibility and will probably be out of the door very quickly.

So, break it down into small parts, don't tell people what you do but the value, outcome, or benefit that you can bring. Reflect back on the purpose of your job on page 130.

For example:

- I keep my clients out of court.
- I save my customers £1,000s of pounds.
- I keep people safe, so they can go home to their families at the end of the day.

- I enable my customers to say "Yes" more often and buy more from us.
- I save lives.
- I feed the general public with healthy food.

Being clear on your value is important

Otherwise known as your Unique Selling Point (USP) or Elevator Pitch. This is because you might only have 10 seconds in an elevator to make the right impact if somebody important gets in and asks you what you do? I'm not sure this ever actually happens, but it's a very good exercise!

What have you got that is different to other people or that sets you apart from the rest? Be brave, be factual, be honest. Just remember to back your value up with real-life examples of your competence and achievements. Don't bluff though — you will soon come unstuck when you are asked further probing questions.

Think of yourself as a limited company. What do you have to offer and how will you add value? How will you prove you are an excellent return on investment so that people will want to do business with you, work with you or have you on their team?

What's your Value?

Example: a plumber charges a call-out fee of £75 to come and fix your washing machine. He's in your house for only five minutes. He hits your machine hard and it immediately starts to work. You challenge him about the fee, telling him it is too expensive for just hitting your washing machine and only being there for five minutes.

How would you reply if you were the plumber?

The plumber considers himself worth his £75 because he knows exactly where to hit the machine owing to his wealth of experience and knowledge.

So, what value do you bring to your clients – what's your expertise?

Creativity – being inquisitive

There are loads of great books out there on creativity, with many useful techniques — it is very worthwhile investing in and exploring such books. However, the greatest catalyst for your creativity is to develop your curiosity.

When you were younger, did you ask a lot of questions and drive your parents mad with your inquisitive mind? Good. All children should be encouraged to ask more questions, especially the "Why?" question.

As we get older, we often find ourselves just accepting things or moaning about them. Stop that –find out why, how, when, who, where and what? Be inquisitive.

Try to read more books and articles, watch more documentaries, become more inquisitive and curious. You will become involved in more conversations (sometimes very random ones) exploring new ideas and concepts. Retain an open mind as to how these new ideas and thoughts might help you; become a sponge and soak it all up.

Looking back, we were at our most creative when we were young children in 'free spirit' mode. This is why I think it is wonderful nowadays to watch young children playing: no boundaries, vivid imaginations, pretend games, and creative minds . As children get older and move into adulthood they become more conforming and routine-focused. I know is necessary at times, but if only we could let them explore more and find new ways of doing things.

Naturally, as children adapt and conform to their environments, so does their thinking as to what they can or shouldn't do.

But what if we all became more inquisitive and asked more questions to help us come up with creative ideas?

Such as:

- What if...?
- How could...?
- Wouldn't it be great if...?
- I have often thought about...?

Follow these statements and questions and see where they take you, try them out, if in doubt, give them a go...you will always learn from the experience.

Notebook page – my great ideas

Every time you have a great conversation or an inspired moment, write it down, otherwise it could get lost forever. Have a page headed 'Great ideas' in your notebook.

Ask great questions

Be the one who asks the best questions rather than the person who does all the talking. Asking great questions is often the difference between doing a good job and a great job. First of all, you need to have the right information from your clients, managers, colleagues and project groups. Don't, as we have already discussed, try to evaluate and solve everybody's problems too quickly. Instead, ask great questions first and when you have all the information, then you can propose your solutions and answers.

After meetings and conversations, undertake some self-analysis and ask yourself whether you should have asked better questions or demanded different information. Don't ask questions just to catch people out or to put them down and make them look silly in front of others.

Ask great questions to improve your understanding so that everybody can do a better job. Listen and listen again... even better, seek to always try to understand (or ask questions to understand) why people think or feel in a certain manner.

If this is a weakness for you, enrol on a coaching course and learn how to be present in conversations, how to help people to create their own understanding of themselves and their own solutions by asking great questions. Pure coaching is all about helping people to solve their own dilemmas and problems by only asking questions and not doing any telling. Try it at work (or out of work) and people will thank you for it.

If somebody does tell you that you ask great questions and always understand the situation before presenting a solution, then say "Well done" to yourself — it's a great art. It shows you care, understand and have true empathy. A wise person knows when not to talk or ask questions — they know what they think and feel but understand that by listening they can then learn more from other people.

If in doubt ask a great question with a; What, Why, When, Where, Who, How and a please tell me some more.

From a Listener to an Understander

You know what you think — try to learn what other people think. Don't listen in order to reply, listen in order to understand. Don't interrupt or cut other people off in mid-sentence, otherwise they will lose their flow and you will lose out on key information and free learning.

The two second rule is a great tip if you happen to be guilty of trying to reply too quickly, thereby interrupting and finishing off other people's sentences. When somebody stops speaking, just pause and give them two seconds to continue before replying.

Being Present in a conversation

Next time you are having a conversation at home or in work, ask yourself whether you are being fully present in the conversation? Is your mind totally focused on what is being said or is your mind off somewhere else? Can you easily remember what has been said and are you able to summarise it accurately and succinctly? Try it and practice being present.

If something else pops into your head, ignore it. Focus on the person talking and what is happening in the room. You will be surprised how much more connected you are to what's going on which people will notice in you. Plus, you will be able to summarise well, which is an excellent assertiveness skill in itself.

Be a leader

Remember, as we have said earlier in the introduction, there is no room for 'them' and 'they' in your vocabulary. And certainly, there is neither the room nor the time in your life to sit around complaining about what other people should or could have done.

My personal view on social media is that it can create campaigners and complainers. It's far too easy to concentrate upon the negatives and say what should have been done or why people haven't done this or done that. If you really want change, you have to get off your backside, leave social media alone and make something happen.

Companies are often full of these types of individuals, always waiting for someone else to make something happen.

So be the person that:

- Asks great questions.
- Comes up with ideas and then say, " I will lead that project."
- Makes things happen.
- Keeps people updated with relevant information.
- Sticks up for what is right and makes a difference.
- Doesn't complain or moan.

Key skills and competences for your future

What inter-personal skills (communication, confidence... etc) or other 'soft skills' do you see as being important to develop in order to meet changing requirements?

For example:

- Leadership or management
- Negotiation or influencing
- Team-building
- Customer Service
- Planning
- Time Management

What technical skills might you need to develop?

- IT Skills / use of CRM packages

- Digital marketing/ social media [look back at 'A Good Starting Point' page 20]

Solicit feedback from your manager, experienced colleagues, or your business network to gather feedback on key areas that are needed for you to develop your career. Ask them where they think you need to develop and improve. Research future job descriptions and roles that you might want to apply for in the future. If your company is willing to invest in training for you, grab the opportunity to review and reflect on your existing skillset and to learn new skills.

Don't treat training as a weakness. Top athletes train every day to better themselves, dancers and actors constantly practice their skills. Treat your career likewise.

If you don't develop your skills, who is going to do it for you?

If you tell yourself, "I am too busy to go on a training course", it is you who will suffer, so get yourself organised and grab the opportunity.

From Expert to Professional

We might be classed as experts in our field of work, but in today's working environment that isn't always enough. We need to be excellent and to be able to get our messages across to our colleagues, managers and clients. They might not have our knowledge, but often these people are key decision makers, so we need to be able to influence them and communicate effectively with them. Being technically good at what you do is one thing, being able to communicate effectively so people listen to you is being a Professional Expert.

Expert	Professional Expert
Technically sound	Gets their message across and understood
Provides the right solution	Packages their service
Makes good decisions	Emotionally intelligent – can access 'gut feeling' when appropriate
Great Knowledge	Creates and adds value
Detailed appreciation of one's subject	Calm under pressure — appreciates others' perspectives

Technical Expert or move into management?

Most technical experts are hardworking, perfectionists and usually with control freak tendencies, but they get stuff done, often by working long hours. They secretly enjoy it though — it's their passion and calling in life.

Often, the only career progression for them is to move up to a management role... but what happens then? The control freak part of their makeup kicks in — "nobody can do it as well as me" — so they end up doing everything themselves. They fail to delegate or empower their teams, so their team members become hacked off and frustrated.

People management isn't easy nor is it for everybody. It's very important that you make the right decision for your career. Very few people leave education and think to themselves, "I want to go and be a manager."

If you are a technical expert, ask yourself whether you can create a career by staying in your current role rather than moving into management, especially if you have a real passion for your line of work. A move into management can often be frustrating for technical experts, as they try to enable and manage a team to do a job that they think they can do better themselves.

Some companies are better at managing this process than others. It should be a key consideration in your career development.

I have worked with many a frustrated technical expert who have ended up as frustrated managers, wishing they were still doing what they had studied and worked hard for in the past.

As my next-door neighbour (who was once a very well-respected and clever doctor before he retired) said to me: "I don't want to spend two days sat in a conference room discussing budgets — I just want to help make people better." He had great passion for his calling as a doctor, and that wasn't to become a manager.

Technology

You can't escape it, so you have to learn to embrace it.

It might not come as naturally to us as it does to the younger generation, but technology has never moved so fast. We can now sit at work and control our heating at home via an app, so why can't we control manufacturing processes and machinery using the same technology? Well we can, and it's already happening.

Take every opportunity to learn about how other companies use technology and how your company can use it and embrace it.

Update your phone and lap top systems when you can and be inquisitive on how to use the latest technology. Go to conferences and participate in webinars to understand more.

What does blockchain or artificial intelligence mean to you? You need to know.

What's the next big thing on the technological horizon and how might it impact your world, your industry, your business and your job?

How does social media work and can you get it to work effectively for your business?

Chapter Five: Proactive Self-Management

If you don't look after yourself, who will?

It is tough out there*, so I need resilience*

but;

I have a plan – *I know my goals and what I want to do*

I am organised *– I manage my time well*

I am self – motivated *– I get the best out of myself*

I am able to think differently *– so I can deal with different challenges*

I work hard to make my ideas and goals happen *– I am always determined*

Focused on what I can control *– I am focused and in control*

Treat your business like a sport

If you play sport, it makes a lot of sense to become as fit as you can in order to demonstrate your natural skill and abilities; you will perform better and enjoy it more. If you sing or play a musical instrument, the more that you practice the better you will become at performing and the more you will enjoy it. Business is exactly the same – the more organised you are, the better you will be able to perform; you will also enjoy yourself more and, very probably, be more successful.

Being able to focus and work on the activities that make the greatest contribution towards your goals will make you more effective, whatever you are trying to achieve. Being organised is an attitude of mind and deciding what you want to spend your time doing is a choice.

Deciding what you do with the 168 hours that you have been allocated each week represents a choice. Do you want to devote all your time to your job and achieve a great career progression, or do you want to work as little as possible in order to just to get by? This is an extreme choice though - being somewhere in the middle might be more appealing.

I have always decided to have a contract between myself and my work — how many hours do I want to give it? Doing so might have prevented me from attaining certain promotions and might have held my career back, but at the same time, it gave the chance to attend every sports day and school play — in other words, it was my choice. When I had fewer domestic responsibilities, I allocated more time and effort to my work and career —this was my choice. Even now, running my own business, I am the one who decides upon the time I am prepared to invest both in and outside of work, but I consider myself very organised so when I am work-focused, I concentrate on tasks that will help me to maximise my potential.

Being proactive in self-management also involves how we start to manage our thinking and get the best out of ourselves. This involves building self-esteem and confidence levels. These are essential skills to Future Proof Yourself and to help with your general wellbeing. Some of us have to work a lot harder than others in developing our confidence and self-esteem, but just as skills can be learned, so can professionalism. We just need to work on our self-esteem and confidence and practice them like any other skill in life. Of course, a good dose of resilience and 'bounce-back-ability' never went amiss! Focusing upon which situations we can and cannot control helps us to stay focused on the tasks, situations and activities that will make us more effective and productive.

If you don't do it for yourself, who is going to do it for you?

Organising myself to make it happen

Personal Self-Management: set & manage both Personal & Career goals

Goal-setting is an activity covered in all aspects of self-development and self-improvement. Does it really work though? Well, that completely depends upon you. Do you have enough desire to make your goals and objectives happen for you, or are you just going through the motions because somebody asked you to set goals for yourself?

If you're very relaxed and like to let life come and go with the view that if it happens it happens and if it doesn't, then that's fine. Just don't get to a ripe old age, then look back and say, "Do you know what, I wish I had done..."

Goals and objectives are very useful and can provide a real sense of purpose if you like to feel the sense of achievement and self-gratification that comes from accomplishing them.

The reason I do this was several years ago my nan died. She was 92 and as they say, 'had had a good innings'. She lived in London throughout the second world war, spending many hours in the Anderson garden shelter during the blitz whilst bombs bounced down the road and onto nearby houses. Meanwhile, my grandad was a bit of a lad; he re-mortgaged the house down at White City and Wembley stadiums whilst betting on dog racing. However, when my nan passed away (the day before my birthday), I am sure she left the world with no regrets. Compared to my upbringing, my nan had had a very tough life, but when she died, she seemed very content, almost as if she had 'done her bit'. Leaving this world with no regrets felt like a great personal gift and started me thinking, "How can I do the same?"

I am very lucky to have a wonderful loving family and enjoy many nice things, but at least twice a year, I sit down and think what I / we would like to do. I write things down that would mean nothing to anyone else but are important to me. I use the heading of Personal Goals in my notebook or on my devices. I think of places to go, people to see, things to do... then I put my lists together and make plans.

I make these lists twice a year; once in the winter around Christmas time, and once in the summer, usually whilst on holiday. I create the time to reflect upon what I have achieved and think about what I would like to do next?

If your job involves having to undertake a Company Appraisal, use this process as a time to reflect and plan. As before, create a page at the back of your notebook to make your lists. When you come up with ideas, it's a good idea to jot them down and review them again in a few weeks — this will help you to decide whether you really want to pursue them. Generating ideas of the goals you want to achieve is a good idea... a very good idea... but remember, it's not a competition — only do the ones you really want to do and which are important to you. If you decide halfway through that you want to do something else, that is fine: "Do what you love and love what you do."

I often set personal goals for myself and then change my mind. Remember, it's not a problem or an issue, it isn't a competition — it's solely for your benefit.

So, grab your notebook and pen, pour yourself a cup of tea or coffee, switch off your mobile device and ask yourself: "What are all the things that I tell myself I would love to do, but never get around to doing?" For example, places to go, people to see, experiences to enjoy... and allow yourself to daydream.

Head up two columns: work goals and personal goals. Then, have three headings: Short-term, Medium-term and Long-term. Reflect and spend time thinking about these. After all, these goals are for you and no-one else can make them happen for you.

	Personal	**Work**
Short-term Six months		
Medium-term		
Twelve to eighteen months		
Long-term Two years plus		

Please feel free to define your own timescales.

It might sound obvious, but to get your goals 'up and running', start at the beginning and focus upon the first small steps. It might be something as simple as having that initial conversation, undertaking some research, or buying a pair of trainers. If you keep your actions small and simple, you will progress more easily and will become more enthusiastic and motivated by your goal.

Now go and award yourself some daydreaming or personal thinking time. Record your ideas — don't evaluate or decide upon them yet — just stop and think about them for a while... but not for too long!

Plan in the steps

Don't try to do everything at once; create simple logical steps, and plan in time to work upon your goals or plans.

Revisit your list of goals on a regular basis. Some people prefer to share their goals since this makes them feel more motivated to achieve them.

For the personal goals that I want to make happen, I focus upon the small steps needed to get the process going, then, enthusiasm, self-motivation and drive begin to take over and, as momentum gains, I find that I am doing things that I really wanted to do all along.

To get your ideas and personal goals up and running might take something as simple as:

- Having a conversation with someone;
- Undertaking some research;
- Making a call to a friend or a contact; or even,
- Creating thinking time regarding what I would like to achieve.

Set a goal to find a goal

"I don't know what I want to do?", is a common refrain. If that is the case, go out and do some thinking and research: talk to people, listen to music, look at art, write things down, walk round a city or take a hike in the country. Go anywhere and to talk to anybody who might be able to inspire you towards your passion and what excites you. Create time to find your passions — people to see, places to go, new experiences, no matter how big or small.

Self-Management / Organisation

Being organised should be an essential starting point. If you're not organised, you will find that you are fighting against yourself before you've even begun.

If you've ever played sport at any level, you'll understand that being fit is a huge bonus and will help you maximise your skills, talents, potential and enjoyment. I was always amazed at how many technically good sportspeople I knew who just didn't put the effort into getting themselves fit and then promptly gave up their sport because they stopped enjoying it. If they had been fitter, they would have enjoyed their sport more and would have performed better.

Fitness is all about effort and an attitude of mind — it's something we can all achieve. The hardest step is usually the first one, getting out of the front door. It's the same as being organised — that's also a choice about effort and mindset. We can all be organised, we can all do it if we choose to, it's just like deciding to be fit.

I must admit, I do admire people who just turn up when they feel like it, without any worries or consideration for others, content in their own time zone or world. Good for them. Being like this — laid-back and chilled — has some benefits if it suits their personality, as long as they never feel afterwards that they've wasted their time or potential.

However, the consequences of such as laid-back attitude can often create problems in the working world — you can't just do your own thing when and how you want; you need to plan and prioritise.

We all have 168 hours a week allocated to us. How we spend those hours is a choice along with planning, communication and the most important one - prioritisation. When you are organised, you will get more done, stay focused, remain more in control and be less stressed.

People often say to me: "I am so disorganised, it's just the way I am." Yes, it is, but it's a choice.

Being organised just makes life easier

Notebooks

Record what you have done and need to do, date your pages and number them — this makes it easier to refer to your notes later. If you lack good memory skills, write it down as it happens.

At the back of your notebook create pages with the headings:

- My ideas
- Personal goals
- Networking list
- What have I learnt?
- Outlook

In business, good time management is essential for keeping track of events, meeting schedules and blocking out time for important tasks so that that people can't 'steal your day'. Try to apply the same concept to your personal life — block out time to make sure you achieve whatever you want to happen.

To Do lists

Make 'To Do' lists at both the start and the end of your working day. Keep asking yourself whether you have everything covered. If you have management responsibilities, ask yourself, "What should I be doing and what could I delegate?"

Kylie Date Time

A good friend of mine had a very lovely girlfriend. However, she split up with him because he was very good at blocking out time to do the really important things in life... in his eyes!

It's fair to say that she was quite high maintenance and enjoyed going out to nice restaurants and clubs. My friend worked long hours as a Finance Director and would come home most nights late, tired and hungry. When he arrived home, he would usually fire up his laptop and keep working whilst eating before falling asleep, much to his girlfriend's annoyance as she wanted to go out. She finally had enough of him when she found out that every other week, he left work at 4.30pm on a Wednesday? Why? Because he had planned it in, blocked out time and let everybody at work know that he was leaving early. He had a season ticket for his favourite football team which was obviously very important to him.

Make things important and block out time. I call it my 'Kylie Date Time'. If Kylie Minogue agreed to meet up with me with at 4pm on a Wednesday for a night out, then yes, I would block out the time and certainly not be late!

Think of it like having bad toothache; you would book an appointment with the dentist, block out time and make sure that you went.

So, decide what is important to you and block out the time: for family, friends, hobbies, or personal reflection time. If you don't do it, then who is going to do it for you?

Silly hours – do you really have to work them?

My daughter's school was close to my wife's workplace. Every morning for five years, my wife would drop her off at 8.45am and get to work for 9:00am. My wife had (and still has) an excellent job as a taxation adviser for a major corporate, but at the end of the day, she was always there to pick my daughter up at 5:00pm on the dot. My wife has worked there for 20 years and has always been very effective in her role and well-respected across the organisation.

My daughter eventually left school to go out to work and my wife now regularly works from 8.15am to 6.30pm. However, is she any more effective as a result? Does she get any more work done? We often discuss this — by working more hours, she doesn't feel as if she is any more effective than when she left work early to pick up our daughter. So the answer is "No"!

Setting up your contract with yourself

It is vital to decide how much time you want to invest in your job or career? If you are happy to work long hours, because you love your job, love the company or want to develop your career as quickly as possible, then crack on and enjoy the journey. However, if more of a work:life balance is important to you, it's time to plan what you want and what you don't want. We have already talked about the hours we work. Start to think about the times when you receive and send emails out of work. Should you set a deadline when you stop sending emails at night, say 7:00pm or whenever you leave work? What about weekends and early morning emails — does this fit in with what you want? Will reading or sending emails late at night or at weekends make you more effective? By all means write them, but don't send them until you are back in 'work hours'. Think about the impact you have on others.

If you work for a company that has peak working times, you will have to accept working extra hours over those periods; e.g. the lead-up to Christmas if you work in retail, year-end if you work in finance... etc. Some professions will have more effect and more of a drain on you and your time than others. Make your decision wisely.

Leaving work on time

If you often find yourself leaving work late, say at 7:00pm every evening, try to aim to leave slightly earlier, say at 6.45 pm. Organise yourself, be assertive, and don't get involved in unnecessary conversations or tasks towards the end of the day. Be assertive and tell your colleagues earlier in the day that if they are likely to need anything from you that day or that week, you will be leaving at 6.45pm. Once you have cracked 6.45pm, try 6.30pm and then 6.15pm — you will get just as much done and be more focused. More importantly, you will create a better quality of life for yourself and the important people around you.

Planning

If you don't make it happen, who is going to do it for you?

Create a way to block out time to do the things that really matter; use a diary, a phone, an app. It doesn't really matter what you use, but block out the time to do what you need to do. We often need to let other people know when we are available and when we are not available. Both at work and at home.

Don't be a dartboard, be the dart player. It's not much fun when people are constantly throwing things at you and expecting you to sort them all out. Be the dart player who is in control of what gets thrown and where it is thrown.

Prioritising

Prioritising is perhaps the most essential tool when coming to managing our time. Doing tasks in the right order is essential to being effective, so always do the tasks first that have the biggest impact on the purpose of your job (what we call 'business critical'). We often procrastinate and prioritise the tasks that we find easy or enjoy most, whilst putting off the most critical tasks. This creates pressure and makes us more ineffective.

Crack prioritisation and life gets easy.

At work, do the tasks that make the biggest difference first. At home, prioritise the activities that make you and your family the happiest. For all the other stuff in life that just needs doing try the following: for administration tasks at work and housework tasks at home, block out time and try to complete them as quickly and efficiently as possible in order to focus upon the important activities and tasks. Try and do them in the evenings and keep your weekends free, if that's what is important to you.

List five things you must do either today or tomorrow.

Now compare the tasks, asking yourself which ones will have the biggest impact or are business critical in your role. Whichever task comes up tops when you compare it against the other tasks is the one you should do first. Number these tasks 1 to 5 in order of importance and complete them in the right order.

Don't attempt your tasks in the wrong order, because you don't like doing certain ones or you are putting off a certain conversation or decision.

Prioritise to make yourself effective and not just efficient

You may be very efficient by having all your emails in neat folders but is that going to make you effective in your day job and help you to achieve your purpose? Always work on the most important tasks first, the ones that make the biggest difference and impact.

Imagine you had to chose only one suit or a dress — which one would you pick to make the biggest impact if you were to go on holiday? If you were a builder or car mechanic and you could only choose one tool for your working day, which one would it be? Or, if you were a golfer and you could only pick one club to play a round of golf with, which one would you choose?

Work in threes

If you have a busy day or a short amount of time to get tasks done, look at your list, pick the top three tasks and focus on those. If you can't get everything done, just make sure that you do the key activities first and retain some control.

Sometimes we just have to accept that we can't get everything done. However, make sure you always carry out your tasks in the right order so you will be effective in what you do.

Being highly effective

For you to be highly effective in your job role, think about what you need to know? This is a very simple concept but is incredibly important. No matter what your work is and what is expected of you, you need to know the following to be able to be effective and be of real value.

To help you out, focus upon six simple words to help you be more effective in your work:

What. What is expected of us is perhaps the best place to start. What does our job role involve and what are we expected to achieve?

How. How should we go about doing our job? How does the business and our managers want us to operate? We need to ensure that we have the right information and training in order to do our job effectively.

When. By when must tasks and projects be completed by? Ban the words 'As Soon as Possible' (ASAP) — what does that really mean? One person's interpretation of ASAP will be different to another's. When work has ASAP attached to it, agree and negotiate a realistic time and date.

Why. Why are we doing this task and how does it fit in with the team and the business? There is nothing worse than doing a job without understanding the purpose of the activity or the desired end outcome. It can be very demotivating.

Where. Where do we need to be in terms of tasks, especially if we are working with other teams and they are relying upon us (or we are relying upon them)?

Who. Who is involved, and who can we go to for help or assistance?

If you have management and leadership responsibilities, how well do your people understand the answers to the What, How, When, Why, Where and Who questions above? if they don't, it's unlikely that anybody is going to be all that effective.

Manage your Manager

If you feel that the answers to the What, How, When, Why, Where and Who aren't clear and your managers, directors and clients are not forthcoming, then you need to ask great questions and learn how to manage upwards.

Managing upwards often puts fear into people. You have to accept that not all managers are as good as they should be, for many different reasons. However, you can help them to be clearer by asking for clarification, so that you can be more efficient and effective, not wasting your time by trying to second guess what they do want.

Be assertive and state what you need in terms of information — this will help you to become more effective and a better performer.

This concept also applies when we are dealing with clients, in order to serve our clients to the best of our abilities by fully understanding their needs, wants and desires.

The concept of What, How, When, Why, Where and Who can be applied to all aspects of our work

Writing an email: this is what we need, this is why and how we need it, this is who it's for and where we need to be by the end of the week and this is when the client needs an answer.

Writing a presentation: this is who we are presenting to and what needs to be delivered. This is why they should listen to us and the benefit they will get. This is when the presentation needs to be delivered and where. Finally this is how we are going to deliver it to knock their socks off.

Delivering on a client project: this is what they want in-terms of the scope and the value they want to achieve, why it's important to their business and who will be the key stakeholders, when its needed and how it needs to be delivered and where.

Just incorporate these simple words into your vocabulary, in terms of explaining what is needed or trying to understand what might be needed.

Don't sit back and expect this information to suddenly appear – you need to go out and obtain it so you can be highly effective and add real value.

Delegation

If you have management responsibilities, delegation is your friend and empowering people should be your style and culture.

Ok, so technically you are great at your job, but you can't do everything. There are only 24 hours in a day and 168 hours a week, so unless you want to spend all of them working, you need to learn to delegate and empower your people. Don't be a control freak; you will suffer and you will not have the time to get on with the important activities that will make a real difference to your role.

Plus, for your own development, if you get bogged down by doing what your team members should be doing, you will not develop your skills and raise your profile higher up in your business. Remember, if you do end up doing your team members' work for them, you will end up as an expensive version of your team.

Take time to reflect on what tasks you can delegate and how you can empower your people. This will free up resources to enable you to put yourself to better use in the business, thereby improving your skills, knowledge and experience and Future Proofing Yourself in the process.

Remember to delegate well — it's all in the communication. Make sure you and your team understand the What, How, When, Why, Where and Who of effective working.

When doing reviews with your people consider the following:

- Are my team fit enough and strong enough to support me?

- Where do they need upskilling?
- What should I be delegating to them?
- What else can I get involved in if I empower and delegate well?
- How can I improve my team's decision-making skills so they don't always need me?
- How can I develop one-to-ones with my team members, so they have the right support to be effective when I am not around?

You can't do everything

You are good... but not that good!

Please remember:

- You are not employed as a manager to do their work — you are employed as a manager to enable them to work.
- You are not employed as a manager to do their thinking — you are employed as a manager to get your team and people to think for themselves.

Build awareness and responsibility. Encourage your people to think for themselves, try to create a more coaching style of management. Train your people well so you can have confidence in them and can leave them empowered and effective.

Be Less Reactive

You can't do everything. So, you certainly can't therefore do everything well. Be more selective and do the things that you do very well and to your highest standards.

Don't get involved in situations and tasks that you don't need to get involved in; you will only cause more stress and poor outcomes. Be organised and undertake activities for a specific purpose or reason. You will enjoy your life and your work more.

What is the purpose of your job?

This is an interesting question. Stop and think — what is the purpose of my job? Not what you do, but the purpose? Why does your company want you to turn up to work each day and why does it pay you a salary?

I run training courses and carry out one-to-one coaching sessions — that's not the purpose of my job, it's what I do. However, 'the purpose of my job' is to develop key people in a business to become more effective and therefore make a greater impact on its organisational objectives, whilst I need to make a profit and enjoy what I 'do'. Most of us need to create value and commercial profit in our roles — profit isn't a dirty word.

And, for those people in non-commercial organisations it might be about reducing costs, risks, creating awareness, improving health, sustainability, reduce risk, wellbeing, working safely, etc.

Having a clear understanding of your purpose is essential in order to be effective in your role.

Remember, being efficient isn't the same as being effective. Being efficient is doing something well; being effective is about completing the tasks and activities that create value and make a difference.

Key Tasks

Think about the five key tasks that you need to undertake to achieve your purpose.

Mine are:

- Deliver Training and Coaching sessions;
- Write Training and Coaching sessions;
- Sell Training and Coaching sessions;
- Develop my team to do the same; and,
- Think differently.

Think about which tasks make the biggest impact to the purpose of your job.

Now the killer question. What percentage of your working day do you estimate is spent on your key tasks and what percentage involves getting caught up in other things (what I call 'stuff')? Think about all those emails, conversations, reports, meetings and procedures — do they really help you to achieve your purpose? Or are they all 'stuff'?

What do you end up doing that doesn't add value? Start challenging yourself and your team, asking: "Why do we do that?", "Does it add value?", "If it doesn't, why are we still doing it?"

What do you think your split is? Key tasks 60% : Other stuff 40%? Be honest with yourself — if you spend 70% to 80% of your time on your key tasks, you are doing well.

What is the Purpose of your Life?

This might seem like a heavy question but try to answer it using the same process.

First of all, think about your definition of 'The Purpose of your Life'. It might be to simply enjoy it and to have fun, to provide for your family, to be a better person, to give more than you take, or to be successful.

However, you need to consider what these definitions really mean to you? This will be particular to you, based upon your values, your upbringing and the way that you think — there is no right or wrong answer.

Then work out which key tasks will help you to achieve 'The Purpose of your Life'. How much time do you spend doing the activities and tasks that help you enjoy your life and which therefore make you happy and successful?

- Have you got your balance right? Do you spend enough time on your purpose and what is important to you? What can you do for yourself to become more organised and to get more things done by being more effective and efficient?
- How well do you manage your use of time?`
- How good are you at prioritising? How could you improve this?
- Do you constantly switch between tasks, or do you always complete one task before tackling the next? If you do find yourself switching frequently, what could you do to focus on an individual task without interruption?
- Do you thrive on being busy doing 'stuff', rather than doing the tasks that give you your purpose? If so, what could you usefully let go of?

Let go of the stuff that is slowing you down!!!

- Thinking
- Behaviours
- Others

- Poor organisation
- Negative thoughts
- Beliefs
- Perceptions
- Attitudes
- Bad habits
- Apathy
- Procrastination

De – Clutter

What is on your mind, buzzing around?

Write a list and prioritise the top three — refocus. What issues and problems do you spend time worrying about? What situations and tasks can you influence and control?

Saying 'No'

Do you find it difficult to say 'No'? What is stopping you? What could you do differently?

As we have said before, you cannot do everything and you can't please everyone. Being able to say 'No' can be difficult. By being better at prioritising, you can be more comfortable in saying: "I need to do other things first before I do what you are asking me to do." This applies to both work and life — do things in the right order, that way you can offer a solution: "I can't do it for you now, but I can help you tomorrow or at the weekend."

Don't be everybody's dartboard. Be the dart player and take control of what gets thrown and where it goes.

Building Resilience

Being resilient involves a whole host of things, but it is primarily about having confidence and what I call 'bounce-back-ability'. It's about being able to deal with situations in a calm and controlled manner, to allow you to perform at the best of your best abilities and be the best version of 'you', no matter what the situation.

One of the key aspects of being resilient is focusing upon things which you can control and not being affected or reacting badly towards things that you can't.

As you will see later in this book, being resilient depends very much upon how you approach situations, about controlling how you think and then applying the right behaviours and actions to those situations. Controlling the controllables and being resilient is about choosing to act and behave in certain ways, whilst not being influenced by others. It is not other people who wind you up or annoy you, it is you who let them wind you up and annoy you.

Think back to when you were a child: did you wind up your brothers and sisters? Or did they wind you up? The only reason you wound each other up was because you could. When either of you stopped reacting badly to being wound up, you then didn't carry on trying to wind them up because it was no longer any fun. This in itself represents a form of resilience: choosing to act in a calm and considered manner.

Building Resilience Takes Practice

Top Ten Tips:

1. Find your core purpose in life - what is REALLY important to you?
2. Practice being a calming influence on others.
3. Know yourself and be clear about your strengths.
4. Pause to think before responding.
5. Build belief in your abilities.
6. Express your emotions through talking, writing or drawing.
7. Look for the learning in every situation.
8. Improve your problem-solving skills.
9. Embrace change.
10. Learn to enjoy the moment.

Exercise

A big factor in being resilient is being able to put your energies into the things which you can control and not becoming side-tracked by things which you cannot control. I often use the phrase: "There is no such thing as difficult people; it's just that we haven't learnt to communicate effectively with them yet."

Think about your reaction to certain situations and reflect whether you could have reacted or behaved differently if you were given the opportunity to relive that situation? You don't want to change your personality traits but, on occasions, we could all benefit from changing our behaviour or how we react to certain situations.

Deciding that we can choose how to act and behave in situations is a big step forward in being resilient.

Think about all the things in life (both in and outside of work) that cause you worry or frustration and think about what aspects you can influence and control. What we can most readily influence and control is our reaction to any given situation.

Examples of the choices we have:

Enjoying your day - it's a choice

Every day when I leave home for work, I decide that I am going to enjoy my day. If I don't enjoy my day, I need to decide what better choices I should make in the future to ensure that I do enjoy my day.

Ask more questions – it's a choice

Take a moment to reflect — might you occasionally be better off asking people questions first to understand how they perceive a certain situation before telling them straight away that you think they are wrong? They might have a different point of view and tell you something that you hadn't thought of before. So, try to ask more questions to gain information before expressing your own opinions and views.

The following statements are worth bearing in mind before airing your own views or assumptions:

- Establish the facts first before making assumptions.
- Do not worry about other people and what they are doing or thinking.
- Understand that you have choices and need to make them for your own wellbeing.

- Ban the words 'them' and 'they' and don't get frustrated by other people's actions.
- If something doesn't quite go your way, what is your Plan B or Plan C?

Being less judgemental towards others or judging others by your own beliefs and values isn't always healthy. Perhaps first understanding their beliefs and values and understanding why they think a certain way might help you to have a much better conversation.

Self-esteem and Confidence

Self-esteem is Latin and means 'self-estimate' – how you estimate yourself?

Do you feel comfortable and confident in all situations? Probably not, so join the club along with most other people. I would comfortably say that nearly every coaching conversation I have with people, not matter who they are, what they have achieved, or what level they are at in their business, self-esteem is the subject that comes up most frequently. This can be for all sorts of reasons, from people's upbringings and their childhoods to the fact they fear failure or that just don't like certain situations.

In my view, being confident and being able to speak well about yourself is essential and professional. During your career you will need to stand up for yourself and present yourself in a positive light. Remember after all, if you can't do it, who is going to do it for you? You can't take your mum along to client meeting or meetings with your senior directors to have her sat in the back ground saying, "Yes, but my son/daughter is very good, and they work very hard."

Here is a challenge and a question for you to consider – how have the last six months or year gone for you?

Do your responses tend towards the positive (what's gone well?) or the negative (what's gone badly?)

Let's focus upon the positive — think of all the things that you have done over the last six months and list:

- What's gone well?
- Difficult situations you have dealt with?
- What have been your strengths?
- What have you been good at?
- Where you have learnt from something going wrong? (Note: there is always a positive in every negative.)
- What have you learnt from something going well?
- What new experiences or responsibilities have you taken on?
- What can you do now that you couldn't do 6 months or a 12 months ago?
- Times you have been outside your comfort zone?
- Times you were nervous, but you survived?

Do you spend enough time thinking about these things? If 'No' then now is the time to start. If you have accomplished something before, then you can do it again, right? Perhaps you have learnt new systems, taken on new responsibilities, presented at important meetings, had new work experiences, or achieved a personal goal.

Write down the answers to these questions and reflect on them, fill your brain with factual positive examples. This needs to become a new way of thinking, so you can help your brain to focus on the positives. It will help you to develop your self-esteem, but it needs work. Think of it like going to the gym to get fit: it needs work on a regular basis, not just every now and then. We need to repeatedly take our brains for workouts with positive factual examples of what we are good at and what has gone well for us.

This will help us to become more confident, because whenever we are faced with challenging situations, we will be able to go into our memory banks and think, "I've experienced a situation like this before." It is then a case of thinking, "I've done this before so I can do it again."

If you are faced with a new challenge, think of all the times in the past that you have faced new challenges and come out of your comfort zone to deal with the situation. Again, it's time to think: "I've done this before, I can do it again."

Confident people have brains that can think and focus on the positive things that have happened, rather than mulling over the negatives. Give your brain the chance to experience positive thoughts – feed it good examples of positive outcomes from your personal experiences.

Comfort Zone Challenges

Think about the last time you went outside your comfort zone? Think about when, where and how it made you feel? Guess what — if you have done it before, you can go outside your comfort zone again. Every time you go outside your comfort zone, ask yourself what did you learn and how did you develop?

Constantly set yourself comfort zone challenges to help grow your self-esteem and confidence and to raise your own levels of motivation. Often the wise people in this world are merely the ones who have just learnt from their experiences and having had lots of comfort zone challenges. If in doubt, go outside your comfort zone and give it a go. You will always learn from the experience.

A three sentence achievement

A great exercise is to write an achievement down in three sentences to help you fully understand and appreciate it.

- The first sentence should be, "What was the achievement?" (What did you do and what was the result?)
- The second sentence: "How did I achieve it?" (What did I do to make it happen and what were the factors that enabled me to achieve it?)
- The third sentence: "What has it meant to me by achieving it?" (What does this now mean to me in terms of confidence and what else can I take on and achieve?)

If you can produce several three sentence achievements, it's good to review them and search for common factors. Did you succeed because of your skills, determination, thinking, creativity, self-organisation, or knowledge? This is a great way to fully understand your strengths and how to play to them in the future.

I can't do it – when did you decide that?

How many times have you heard yourself saying, "But I can't do that"? All good coaches will respond: "When did you decide that?" This is a question that we should ask ourselves on a regular basis.

When did you decide that? Where is the proof or the facts? Often there aren't any, so how about changing your thought process to, "It's going to be a challenge, but I have overcome other challenges in the past, so I could give this one a go... should it not go to plan, at least I'll have learnt from the experience."

So, if in doubt, give it a go.

Being able to present both yourself and your achievements is an essential aspect of Future Proofing Yourself. Clients will at some stage ask you: “What can you do for us?” Senior managers might ask: “Why should we give you this job to you?”

Be confident about what you are all about. Being able to feel confident and having good self-awareness will help you to make better decisions, get more done, inspire others and help you to enjoy being ‘you’.

Go and practice it, because if you don’t, who is going to do it for you?

Chapter Six: Developing a Clever Way of Thinking

Don’t just think like you do

I know how I think and what I know, but what advantages would I have had if I understood what other people thought and knew?

Naturally people in our working environments all communicate in different ways, they like information in different formats, people are motivated by different values and see the same situation from different viewpoints, so naturally people think differently. On the whole we know how we think, but how do others think and make decisions.

If we can learn to think differently and understand how other people communicate, we can open up more opportunities for ourselves and find it easier to communicate, influence and negotiate with other people. You don't have to always agree with other people, but we can understand why they think that way.

Naturally we are now faced with a new way of thinking in our businesses with young adults looking at the world, work and business from a different perspective. It's easy to dismiss their ways of working and thinking but remember they are the future and will become our customers, colleagues, managers and leaders for the future, learn to adapt or miss out on future opportunities.

Managing our own thinking can have a hugely positive impact on ourselves and the way that we work and operate. In a world of social media and marketing, people constantly wanting us to feel we are missing out and someone else has got a better deal in life because they have purchased superior products to us or have more fun.

In the working environment learning to think in an entrepreneurial way or like your directors and senior managers will help you communicate more effectively. Knowing how your clients think and make decisions and how certain markets are changing their perceptions and thinking will help you to keep up to speed and one step ahead of the game.

On an individual basis do our thinking processes help or hinder our progress? Are we first to see the problem that will hold us back or the opportunity that will drive us forward? Learning to think differently can be challenging and hard work but like any other skill set it takes practice.

Even if what I am working on goes wrong, it's not a disaster, don't over react. Remember you have had a new experience and have the opportunity to learn which can help you in the long run when faced with similar situations.

Learning to look at situations from a different perspective will help you to learn more, have more opportunities and see the potential in your future. Spending time with people who have the ability to see the opportunity rather than the obstacles can help you to maximise your potential and progression.

How we think can, along with most things, be a choice. If you leave the house in the morning determined to enjoy your day you are more likely to seek the opportunities to enjoy it. Rather than thinking, "Here we go again — it's a different day but it's the same old xxx."

If you have a challenging day ahead of you, just think, "Right this is my opportunity to show myself and others how good I am and I am up for the challenge."

Remember the reality is never as bad as the perception in life, learn to manage your thinking to aid and benefit yourself.

Creating inspiration to think differently is another activity we can work on rather than thinking 'but I am not very creative'. Focus on where and who makes you think differently. Work at it and find people and places that inspire you. Don't wait for them or they or others to do it for you. Go and explore new environments and work hard to be more inspired, creative and thoughtful.

If you don't do it for yourself who is going to do it for you?

Thinking differently

'Who' makes you think differently?

This is an important exercise if you are looking for ideas and inspiration.

Create a list of people who you feel think differently to you, who are able come up with alternative ideas to you, and who are able to see situations from a different perspective. You don't have to always agree with them, but if they have the ability to think differently, this can be inspiring and help you to be more creative.

Try to understand why they think the way they do and how they have arrived at their ideas and conclusions. Ask yourself:

- Do you spend enough time talking to them?
- If not, give them a ring and have a chat with them.

The people who can help you to think differently could be the younger members or more mature members of your family, or somebody from a completely different background with different experiences.

Look at your network and decide upon the key people who can inspire you and spark your imagination. These people can be invaluable when you come across a situation that you are not sure how to deal with or a problem that you haven't experienced before.

We all know how we think and how we see things. However, to open our minds up to new ways of thinking and new ways of doing things, or to go and spend time finding out what other people think, can be very inspiring.

Never be afraid to ask. Most people really appreciate it when you ask for their advice as they will feel honoured that you value and trust their opinions.

'Where' makes you think differently?

It's not just people who can make us think differently. "Motion changes emotion", as the saying goes, so get out there and experience different environments:

- Walk the dog early in the morning.
- Go to a concerts, a play or wander round an art gallery.
- Experience the view by the sea or up a mountain.
- Experience the roar of a sporting crowd.
- People-watch from a café table.

Work out what works best for you. We all need a bit of help sometimes, so try to regularly experience different environments that can inspire you.

Controlling the Controllable

How often do we worry about things over which we have no control? How often do we make judgements about people and situations, but by being judgemental, we can often create negativity in our own minds which can impact either the situation or people close to us?

Do we often invest too much energy into situations that can have a negative impact upon us and others? Usually, we are the only person who suffers when we put too much energy into a negative situation. Spending time worrying about things over which we have no control or blaming others will only create negativity in our own minds.

List out what causes you worry and concern

What can you control? The answer is our reaction to any given situation. We can choose how we deal with these situations in either an angry aggressive manner or a calm manner (sometimes easier said than done!) However, if we can learn to manage our own behaviour and deal with situations in a calm manner, this is a wonderful trait. Keeping calm whilst everyone around you is losing their heads takes practice. It is worth the effort though, both in terms of your own wellbeing and in terms of the respect from others who then come to regard you as a calm person under pressure.

Think of situations when you have become frustrated or reacted badly. If only you could change your thinking and behaviour, how much more enjoyable would your life become? If only you didn't get so wound up in the first place? What situations or people which trouble you, do you need to think differently about?

"If you don't like something,

change the way you think about it."

This is a great outlook to have but it requires practice. Improving your thinking habits and not being overly impacted by negative situations will improve both your resilience and your well-being.

Always have a Plan B so when things do go wrong or when the inevitable happens, you will have a back-up plan which enables you to stay in control and not be too negatively impacted.

When the going gets tough

When the going gets tough, that's when the real 'you' needs to turn up.

We can all perform well when business and markets are easy, or when we only have to turn up to acquire new business, customers love us and we can do no wrong, the economy is booming. Life is easy and money flows in.

However, what happens when there is a downturn in the economy? How well do you perform under pressure when deals need to be done because the rest of the business is relying upon you? The best time to really show your real value and qualities is when markets are tough.

In these circumstances, calmness under pressure and working with a clear mind is essential,. Being confident, proactive and leading from the front is how we get to show our true worth. If you can be successful under tough conditions, you can keep yourself Future Proofed for almost any eventuality.

There is a lovely phrase: "Do you just turn up and participate, or do you turn up and contribute and make things happen?" Be your own leader and make things happen.

Flip it or Reframe it

These are great techniques that we can all employ, but they do take some practice. If you have negative thoughts running through your head, try to park those thoughts and focus on a positive outcome from the situation.

"If you don't like something,

change the way you think about it."

Negative situation	**Positive response**
It's cold and wet when you are walking home.	"That cup of tea or bowl of soup will taste "twice as nice."
You run into a traffic jam or your train is delayed.	"I can make that call on hands free or read my favourite book."
You've lost your phone.	"This gives me time to take back control of my life and some much needed peace and quiet, rather than being controlled by my phone."
Your friend has cancelled tonight.	"Great! I'll watch that film I've always wanted to watch."
You have been left to present on your own.	"What a fantastic opportunity!"
You have been left to sort everything out on your own.	"This is an opportunity to show people what I am capable of."
A client has gone mad at you.	"If I can deal with that situation, I can deal with anything."
People never want to talk to you.	"I have approached other people before and started up conversations with them which has worked well."

How can you create the right mindset for you? It takes practice.

Every time you have a negative thought, either when you are trying go to sleep or when you are on your own, think what the positive might be in that situation? This does take time.

It's often the same negative thoughts that reoccur in our minds. Write down your thoughts and then think about the positive outcome or the positive way forwards from the situation.

Positive thoughts

Creating positive and realistic thoughts will have a considerable impact upon your well-being and 'Future Proofing': you will get more done and people will want to work with you.

"There is no such thing as bad weather,

only inappropriate clothing."

If it snowed and you went for a walk in the snow wearing flip flops, shorts and a t-shirt, that wouldn't be very enjoyable, would it? However, if you had good boots, a thick jacket, gloves and a hat, you would enjoy the walk and the environment around you.

"There are no such things as difficult people,

it's just that we haven't learnt to communicate with them effectively."

If you have the right communication skills, you can deal with almost any type of difficult situation. If you have the right mindset, you can manage your own behaviour instead of reacting badly to another person's behaviour. People communicate in different ways and view situations from different perspectives. If you can learn how to deal with all different styles of communication and get on with everyone, life just becomes so much more enjoyable.

"It's a shame they are unable to express themselves effectively;

I can help them get their message across."

Instead of criticising or enjoying someone struggling, perhaps you can help them and support them in their communication?

Focus upon what is important to you

Reflection time is essential to think about what you want to do and what you want to create, both for yourself and for those people who are important to you.

Life can become very busy, but we always seem to try to pack more and more in as our lives evolve. We seem to be addicted to filling every moment of our days on-the-go and doing stuff.

Depending on your age, reflect on what your parents or grandparents' life might have been like when they were your age? Is your lifestyle any better? Think about what you have compared to what they had and talk to them about it — it's a very interesting topic. Who is, or was, better off?

I suppose that depends on your measurement of 'better off'?

- Money/ wealth
- Time
- Material things
- Contentment
- Stress levels

What is really important to you and do you spend enough time on it? Do you get sucked in to feeling certain things are important to you, but upon deeper reflection they just distract you from what is really important? Remember, there are only 168 hours in a week — do you spend yours wisely and are you getting the balance right?

Limiting beliefs

At some point in time, we have all either said to ourselves, or heard somebody else say: "I can't do this", or "I'm not very good at that." A question often posed in response by Life Coaches is, "When did you decide that you couldn't do that?" or , "When did you realise that you weren't very good?"

It's a great question to ask both yourself and other people to challenge your/their limiting beliefs. We all have limiting beliefs — they have a negative impact upon us maximising our potential, they hold us back in life.

So what are the facts, where is the proof that you can't do something? I expect there are often no facts, there are only limiting thoughts in your head. Have you really tried and worked hard to overcome that limitation? Often, the answer is "No". Have you asked for help and set yourself a plan to overcome that limitation? Once again, the answer is often "No."

For example, since I was 16 years old, I have wished that I could speak French. So, 30 years on, have I addressed this wish, can I speak good French? Unfortunately not, because I keep telling myself that I am not very good at languages and I will never be able to do learn French. And I am correct — with that attitude and way of thinking it's never going to work!

However, I have had a completely different attitude towards other things in life, and with a positive attitude I have been successful in achieving what I have set out to do.

"Whether you think you can or can't, you will always be right."

Henry Ford

This quote from Henry Ford is so true. Time then to reframe, "I can't do that", or "I'm not very good at that", to, "I'm working on it and I have a plan to achieve it", or, "I have decided to focus my efforts on other areas that I will enjoy more." Remember, it's all about choices — Make Positivity your choice.

Enjoy what you have got

Future Proofing Yourself and creating your own sense of wellbeing is about remaining in control and focusing on the things that are important to you. Here are some positive thoughts to help you enjoy what you already have and which will make a difference to your outlook:

- Have time with important people.
- Have time doing what you enjoy.
- Just enjoying the moment.
- Enjoying your children when they are young.
- Don't dream of a Friday on a Monday.
- On a Monday dream of the opportunities ahead.
- Love the environments you enjoy being in.
- Enjoy the smell of the air outside.
- The beauty of nature.
- Love life and don't wish it away, enjoy every moment.

One look at social media can be enough to drive anyone into a fit of jealousy, seeing friends and acquaintances living their 'perfect lives'. However, is the grass always greener in somebody else's life? I doubt it, it's just our perception playing tricks with us and our negative thoughts dragging us down.

Enjoying the moment

When was the last time you sat down and just enjoyed a simple pleasure and said to yourself this is great?

- A chat with friends.
- A cup of tea outside.
- Reading a magazine or a book.
- Standing under an umbrella in the pouring rain.
- Listening to inspiring music.
- Enjoying a joke.
- Really looking at a picture and taking in all of the detail.
- Walking in a city, admiring the architecture and thinking about its past history.

Challenge yourself every day to think of at least one moment when you can stop and think to yourself: "This is really good — I'm so pleased that I'm here." Don't feel you have to take a picture of the moment and share it on social media though — just enjoy the moment for yourself!

I have never understood why parents spend all their time watching their children's school plays and events through a camera lens. Get one person to record it and share it so that everybody else can enjoy the moment.

Enjoy the moment by being present; in other words, give your undivided attention to a person or a situation and don't start thinking about the other things you might need to be doing. Stop rushing about; you aren't that important that other people can't cope without you. Not everything needs to be done today; prioritise and do one thing at a time — less juggling, more enjoying. Eat and drink more slowly; it's not going to run away; you are not in a competition as to who can eat the fastest.

Reduce that Ego

If you have a large ego, manage it and be aware of the impact it can have upon you and other people. With an inflated ego, you can set yourself unrealistic standards and expectations which you are then unable to match and then proceed to beat yourself up, causing yourself stress and worry in the process. The impact of your ego upon others is that they will not want to work with you, feeling it's all about 'you' — this is not a good place to be.

Learning - Looking for inspiration

I remember being back at school as a teenage with a teacher who was getting very irate with her rowdy class (which I expect I contributed greatly to!) She shouted at everybody: "I'm looking for some peace and quiet and sensible behaviour." As she said this, she opened a drawer in her desk. With great comic timing, my friend Mark shouted out: "Well you won't find it in there", much to the amusement of everyone in the room.

Finding inspiration and motivation involves opening up your mind to new ideas and ways of thinking. 'Self-inspiration' doesn't just happen, you won't find it in a cupboard or a drawer, you can't go and buy a bottle of inspiration on the internet... if only!

So where do we find inspiration? The answer is everywhere. We need to expose our minds, eyes and bodies to more of life's experiences:

- Talk to more people who think differently to us.
- Watch films that inspire us.
- Enjoy music with messages that give great meaning.
- Go walking, by the sea, mountains or anywhere that gives us a sense of passion and good feelings.
- Go cycling, running or swimming.
- Take up art, or go to an art gallery or museum.
- Go to a sporting event and experience atmosphere from the crowd to inspire us.
- Sit in a field or a wood to experience nature.
- Walk the streets of a city and feel the 'busyness'.

Find out where and what inspires you; it makes finding future inspiration a lot easier.

Self-Talk

Negative self-talk can cause problems by creating self-doubt.

Do you find yourself worrying about an upcoming event, a challenging conversation, difficult meeting, traveling somewhere new, being on your own, or having to talk to others? Try to remember, you have overcome these situations in the past, so you can do it again. Alternatively, if it's a first time, look upon it as a great opportunity to learn with a new experience.

Think about things that have gone well and (even if they haven't gone so well), and what have you learnt from the experience? By learning from an experience, there is always a positive in every situation even it didn't go too well.

Notebook page

Write down in your note book the positive things that you have achieved and the topics that remind you of these positives. Then, when you need a bit of help, turn to the relevant page and read your positive thoughts. Tell your worries and concerns to take a hike because you want to think about something positive instead.

Reality is never as bad as your perception

We often perceive the worst and make ourselves nervous about doing something or going somewhere. The reality is that when we do get there or do it, the experience is almost never as bad as we thought it would be. It might be a meeting at work with our directors, a pitch to clients, a difficult conversation coming up, or a challenging few weeks of heavy workload.

At the end of our working day, we should reflect on how well it went. If we do so, we will soon realise that all the anxiety and worry present at the start of the day soon disappeared. We can we learn from this, we can learn how to embrace new opportunities and challenges rather than fearing them. As the saying goes, *"The reality is never as bad as the perception."*

Think about a time recently when you have been nervous about a meeting, interview or a presentation. Then after it was over you think to yourself, that wasn't so bad after all was it?

Every topic in this book will only work if you adopt a positive proactive approach together with a positive mindset. It just needs practice though — it's no different to learning to run two miles for the first time or learning to cook or learning to play a musical instrument. So, start to self-manage your positive thoughts so that you can enjoy life more.

Think of somebody in your network who has overcome a tough situation in life and has managed to turn negative situations into positive ones. Go and talk to them and ask them how they have coped.

We all need help in Future Proofing Ourselves, but we need to start this conversation ourselves.

New generation experiences: "Well in my day..."

Nowadays, the generations at work have never been so diverse. We have all sorts of names for the different generations: Generation X, Y, and Z, plus Baby Boomers and of course, The Millennials. Don't worry about the names and labels given to all the different generations (they can become rather confusing), it's what can you learn from them that is more important. Try to understand how they think and behave without becoming bogged down by stereotyping.

Think about your working environment: think about the cultural diversity and age diversity present there. You have to learn to communicate with different people who communicate in different ways:

- How do they think?
- Why do they think that way?
- What can you do to understand their way of thinking?

- How will business and people make decisions in the future?

We need to be especially mindful of the younger generation coming in to the workplace for the first time, to understand their energy, their openness to communicate and their relaxed approach to 'standard' business and working practices.

The younger generation often have great ideas and new concepts. One thing they do like is to understand the 'Why?' which I think is particularly positive; why do we do it that way and is there a better way? Often the answer is "Yes", which enables us to stay ahead of our competition.

Embrace this way of thinking to help yourself understand how we might all be working in the future. Back in the day, your way might have been great, but we should reminisce carefully so as not to blur our vision for the future.

There is now a lovely concept at work called Reverse Mentoring. Mentoring has traditionally been about a more experienced and knowledgeable person supporting and guiding a less experienced person into the world of working. Reverse Mentoring flips this round so that the younger, less experienced person guides the more experienced one towards new ideas, technologies, ways of working and, most importantly, new ways of thinking. Just to stand still in our business and working environments, we need to develop, learn and think differently to survive. So go and ask a young enthusiastic person to mentor you — it's well worth the investment.

Chapter Seven: Being in Control of Your Well-Being

It's much more enjoyable that way

Make life easier for yourself – make sure that you enjoy it

One life, one body. Try and look after both of them, because if you don't...

Learning to understand your body and how it performs to the best of its ability is a form of professionalism. There are many factors that impact us physically and how we operate; investing time in understanding these factors and making the right choices will be time well spent and will help us to maximise the impact we can have in our working careers.

Working on being happy and content with life, despite all the difficulties and challenges that it can throw at us, is the best way to start creating our own well-being.

Working and dealing with pressure is an essential skill in Future Proofing Yourself so you can perform to the best of your abilities in all situations. We can all be good at what we do when the working environment is relaxed and non-pressurised but, as we are well aware, the more responsibilities and pay that we are afforded, the greater the expectation upon us to perform and produce results. Being able to work in pressurised situations should be seen as a positive opportunity to demonstrate that you are good at what you do and will be able to step up and perform when the pressure is really on. The better you can manage your reaction to pressure, the happier and more content you will be. You will become more relaxed and in control of your well-being.

Our well-being is strongly influenced by our financial position, which in turn, is dictated by the choices and decisions we make in managing our money. Everybody has a different relationship with money. Try to put into context what you do have in order to help you have a better relationship with your financial situation — enjoy what you have, rather than feeling frustrated by what you lack in life.

Enjoy being you and enjoy what you have got. Life is not a competition against other people. Don't measure yourself with what other people might have in terms of materialistic items.

Well-being...or what really matters in life – Getting the balance right

Health

Eating and Drinking – Nutrition

We are what we eat. Our nutrition makes a huge difference to our performance and well-being... although you don't need another lecture from me on what to eat and drink or what not to eat and drink...but don't overdo the drinking either! All I would say is research and find out what is best for you, create a plan and then stick to it.

Thinking about how we want to perform at work and develop our potential can often be impacted on what we eat and drink so we can perform to the best of our abilities. You can't expect to be alert, focused and to perform well in meetings or important work events if you have eaten and drunk the wrong things beforehand. If you want your body and brain to perform well, if you want to have stamina and to be alert, then you need to invest in what you put inside you.

Sleep

Sleep has a major effect on our everyday performance. One way to help ourselves perform is by being aware of the time of day when we work best. Are you more on-the-ball and switched-on in the morning or in the afternoon? Or is it late in the evening when you work at your best? Again, spend time deciding what works best for you. I wish I had been born in Spain — I find that a siesta in the afternoon is a great way to re-energise myself, whether I am travelling or working from home.

I am a morning person — I prefer to get up early and start work at say 6:30am or 7:00am. I try to prioritise tasks that require my full attention and concentration for the morning, and schedule more interactive tasks (such as meetings) in the afternoon when my energy levels can drop and the buzz of dealing with people re-energises me. I then enjoy working late afternoons and early evenings, but I really struggle to work late into the night — I become very tired and want to switch off, so carrying on working past that time becomes totally unproductive. I love going to bed early, at say 9.30pm to 10:00pm so I can chill and totally switch off. Other people might have a totally different working day — figure out what's best for you and your particular working environment.

Alternatively, think what type of working environment might complement your particular energy levels. You might prefer a working environment where it doesn't matter when you get the job done as long as it gets done, where you can work whatever hours you wish. This can create a great lifestyle for those people who don't want to work a 9-to-5 routine. You might want to work in an environment where you start early and finish early?

However, be careful if you are working for an American company whilst living in the UK and you like finishing early... forget it, as the US is just coming online as you clock off in the UK! At the other end of the scale, if you don't like early mornings and your business has also got offices or clients in the Middle or Far East, it's not going to work well for you as you will probably be expected to be present online and available for meetings in the early hours of the morning. And if you really value your sleep, working for an Australian company might cause you more than a few problems!

Time for family and friends

Do you ever look at yourself through the eyes of your friends and family? Are you a good son or daughter to your parents? And good brother or sister to your siblings? Are you a good partner to your better half as the saying goes? What about how your children see you?

I ask my wife twice a year, "How's your husband doing?", normally at dinner on our wedding anniversary and on her birthday. Sometimes she replies positively, which allows me to sit back and smile and think, "Well, everything is ok then." However, sometimes she replies more critically and I think, "That's a bit harsh!". However, I try to stay calm, not get defensive and ask her for examples to allow me to see the situation through her eyes and make any necessary changes.

I also ask my daughter, "How is your Dad doing?" This can be a bit more challenging as I would often love to know what she is thinking, how she saw the world as a teenager previously and now, how she views it as a 20-year-old young woman. Again, she often says things that set me thinking, so I can go away and reflect upon how I might improve and be a better Dad for her.

Unless we take time to reflect and understand how others see us, we will miss out on opportunities to improve those relationships and make more of a positive impact on those people closest and most important to us.

But I hear you say, "Why is it always about me having to change?" To which my answer would be, "I can't change another person's behaviour, only my own". So, if I want to have better relationships, I will need to work a bit harder at adapting and understanding how other people see things. We can, of course, give them feedback, our feedback on their behaviours or, even better, give them a copy of this book. Choices choices!

Friends

Would you like to have 'you' as a friend? Are you a good friend? Do you give more than you take?

Of course, we need to make sure that we don't get taken for granted or spend all of our time running around trying to please everyone else. Sometimes it's good to please ourselves first and not to try to solve everyone else's problems. As you have no doubt discovered, it simply cannot be done.

So are you:

- A good listener?
- Reliable and turn up on time?
- A person who does things when you say you will?
- Supportive and understanding?
- Somebody who doesn't try to 'add value' to all conversations and interrupt others in the process?

A good friend of mine recently asked me; "How was your holiday to Australia with the family?"

I told them that we loved it and mentioned a few places that we went to which we really liked, but my friend then interrupted me and asked if I had been to some other places which I hadn't mentioned. We hadn't, so he then spent the next 20 minutes telling me where we should have gone and what we had missed out on. By the time he'd finished, I wished he hadn't asked me about my holiday, because he hadn't appeared the slightest bit interested. He just wanted to talk about where he had been; it was not a two-way conversation.

Remember the previous chapter with the example about the church... how we should spend more time understanding how others see things and what makes them tick? I realise that it takes patience and energy to attempt this, but if we want to improve ourselves there is going to have to be some pain; it's no different to training to do 50 press-ups or learning how to play a new piano piece. It doesn't always come easy. Reflect upon your values, how would you like people to see you and how would you like to see your yourself and start from there.

Passions - Exercise – Music – Art – Cooking - Singing - Reading - Watching great films

How do you lose yourself? Is it in a passion or something you really enjoy doing? We all need to escape at some time, and just doing more of the things that we love doing can make a real difference to our well-being.

I love the outdoors, especially walking and cycling. I like going off on my own and feel I am a better person when I do these things on a regular basis; I'm far more relaxed and tolerant upon my return. What are your passions? Where can you lose yourself and make sense of the world around you?

Create some 'You' time

As we have already noted, looking after ourselves in body and mind helps us to be a better version of ourselves and therefore, a better family member or friend. Remember you can't do everything, and you can't please everyone — sometimes you need to stop and put yourself first. This in turn will make you a better 'you' and better for the people who are important to you. We all have our faults; learning to manage them is a hugely positive step to Future Proofing Ourselves.

Stop

I am in hurry and I don't know why
I'm in a hurry to get things done
Oh, I rush and rush until life is no fun
All I really got to do is live and die
But I'm in a hurry and I don't know WHY
Step back
Think
Organise your thoughts
Proceed in a controlled manner

Randy Vanwarmer / Roger Murrah

Why are we always in a hurry? Do you ever get to Monday morning and wish it was Friday afternoon? Do you get to Friday afternoon and you think, "Thank goodness that week is over!" Why? Why should we want to wish our lives away? Enjoy the journey, embrace the learning.

Make time for yourself each and every day, promise yourself you are going to enjoy your days and weeks. No more wishing your life away. If you don't enjoy it, what changes can you make to ensure that you do?

Notebook page

Along with your personal goals, note down what you have a passion for and love doing. How can you create the habit to make these things more important to you and give them the time you deserve? It can be something as simple as reading a book or a paper, listening to music, catching up with certain people, going for a walk, chatting to your dog or cat… or even someone else's dog or cat! If you feel your life is too complicated and too busy, reflect upon how you can simplify it.

Our brains can't cope

My colleague has a wonderful untested theory. For many millions of years, human beings only had to worry about keeping themselves, warm, fed and protected. That meant planting seeds, watching their crops grow, harvesting them, collecting fruit and berries, catching animals to eat... etc. Then, along came modern-day living and our brains started to struggle to cope. Are we overloading them, causing our bodies to respond with illnesses and stress? In which case, could we keep ourselves fresher and on top of our game by keeping our lives simpler and giving our brains a rest?

A sportsperson can't keep training their muscles constantly, otherwise they will wear out and fatigue will set in. Could fatigue be the next issue in generations to come? We have the chance to live longer with new medicines and advances in science, but will our brains be so fatigued that our quality of life will be severely reduced? Furthermore, if we are having to work longer and longer, what state will our brains be in? How will you keep your brain fresh and fit?

Bouncebackability

Bouncebackability is how you pick yourself up when you're feeling low or have suffered a setback. It's a great phrase, but it's not always as easy to do it as it is to say it. Sometimes it's good to curse, go off, sulk, get in a mood and wallow in a bout of self-pity. But then it's time to say enough is enough — when the going gets tough, the tough get going and it's bouncebackability time!

The first thing to consider when you stay in self-pity mode for too long is who will suffer the most? Yes, it's you. Those around you will become annoyed with you, but in the end, it's you that will suffer the most.

What can you take as a positive from the situation so you can learn for next time? Don't start blaming others — remember that life is about choice, so what can we learn from the situations that put us in a grump and a bad mood?

- How can a bad situation be turned into a positive?
- Can the experience make you a better person?
- Can you put it down to a life experience?

Ask yourself how you have dealt with a disappointment before? How did you bounce back? If you have done it before, you can do it again. It might be a good time to sit back and reflect upon the good things that you have got, rather than the things you haven't?

If you are in a work environment and you are having a tough time:

- Can this experience make you stronger?
- Think about what you have achieved and that you have worked hard to get to where you are today.
- If you are in a position of responsibility, it's going to be tough, but perhaps it's time to show people what you are made of?

So, if today's a bit rough, remember you usually have a lot more good days than bad ones. However, if you don't, then ask yourself what can you change? Don't start to compete with other people on who has been dealt the hardest hand in life or who has the toughest, most pressurised job. There is only one winner in those conversations and it's negativity.

Managing pressure at a high level

I was asked to run a Managing Stress & Pressure course for the senior partners in a firm of accountants. In my experience, audiences like this are often slow to warm up, with participants taking a while to share their thoughts in front of their fellow partners. So, I thought I would open the course in a slightly different manner and take a bit of a risk in order to get the course up and running quickly with everyone participating.

I addressed the audience as follows:

- You have all studied for many years to reach the position of partner.
- You have all worked very long hours to hit client deadlines, such is the culture of your industry.
- You have billed your clients hundreds of thousands of pounds (one partner interrupted me and said, "More than that!")
- I think it's fair to say you all enjoy a large salary and receive generous performance-related bonuses.
- You probably drive expensive cars, dine at some of the best restaurants and return home in the evening to larger-than-average houses.

They all agreed, so I continued:

- Some of you have reached the pinnacle of your careers (this got a few laughs!)
- Didn't you think that working at this level as a partner would involve dealing and managing pressure against challenging client expectations?

They started to talk as a group and most of them admitted that they had never thought like that and were very fortunate. Sometimes, the best way to accept a situation is to look at it from a different perspective.

We proceeded to cover many of the topics that are outlined in this book so that they could self-manage and make necessary changes to continue to perform at partner level without suffering burn-out.

Enjoy what you have got

What really matters in life?

Three friends in a pub

Three friends were having a well-earned drink in a pub after work on a Friday evening.

The first friend said, “My goodness, I’ve had a tough week. I’ve been here, there and everywhere. The traffic has been horrendous, and my working days are getting longer and longer — I don’t know where it’s going to end?!”

The second friend replied, “That’s nothing. My working days are a lot longer than yours. I hardly ever get to see my kids, and when I do eventually get home, I have to deal with more emails on my laptop. It’s just constant with no let-up!”

“You two don’t know you’re living”, interjected the third friend, “I do all of that and more. Every Saturday morning and Sunday afternoon I have to respond to work demands, it’s just never-ending. I am so tired and worn out.”

A fourth friend then enters the bar. The first three friends all ask how his week has been and the fourth friend replies with a big smile on his face: ”It’s been brilliant thanks! Business is great with lots of exciting projects coming up. I went out for a lovely dinner last night and am really looking forward to going away this weekend.”

"It's all right for some isn't it...for those who of us have an easy life?!", replied one of the first three friends.

Discussion point

What sort of lives have we created for ourselves when we have to start competing on how stressed we are, as the first three friends did in the example above? And for the fourth friend with an 'easy life', well perhaps that friend had organised and planned it that way?!

It's very easy to end up in a routine; you get up early to go to work and beat the traffic, to get ahead of the game and to be organised.... get loads done and work through lunch. Then, suddenly it's 6:30pm and you wonder where has the day gone? Time to eventually go home, but first just finish a couple more things off. Finally you get home, have something quick and easy to eat, deal with a few more messages... have a few snatched home and family conversations with reminders not to forget this that and the other, before finally getting to bed. However, it's not long until the alarm clock goes off again!

Great, it's the weekend, but you're knackered. You were going to the gym, to see friends and do stuff around the house. They can wait... I'm so tired. Damn, it's my mum's birthday and I've forgotten, I'd better not lie around. Great, it's Sunday... relax, watch a bit of telly and some cookery programmes... but I need to get that presentation sorted for Monday morning... always be ahead of the game... I think!

The alarm goes off!

Time to act

We have mentioned before in this book that there are 168 hours a week... and still we can't organise ourselves well enough to spend two hours at the weekend doing something we really enjoy?!

Being effective in work is obviously very important but what about being effective outside of work? The happier we are outside of work, doing the things that will bring us and our family value and enjoyment, will help us enjoy our work more.

I appreciate that for a lot of people who have family and relationship commitments, just dropping everything when we want to enjoy ourselves can seem a bit selfish. Hence, packing our bags at short notice and going off trekking across the Himalayas will have consequences. However, having taken on various commitments and responsibilities, try to be realistic about what you can and can't do. But remember these all involve a sequence of choices. I do accept that when people have been dealt a difficult hand in life, choices can be limited, but how we deal with what has been dealt to us is always a choice, no matter how harsh that might seem.

Middle-aged men with no hobbies or interests

It has often been said women generally outlive men because they have more hobbies, friends, interests and keep their minds and bodies more active. Often men focus solely upon work, work, and work. They have to provide, and their ego often prevents them from giving up their career, their status, their cars and their salaries, etc.

We all want and need to be valued, to have self-worth, to have a sense of motivation and achievement. However, it's not just through work that we can achieve these motivation values.

So stop being boring — go and find other interests, make friends, get involved in local organisations. Getting the balance right in the long-term is more beneficial. Learn to let go of your work, to create new beginnings, journeys and adventures and become interesting again. Women are much better at doing this; they often have more friends, a better social life and create a more purposeful lifestyle by getting involved.

Think of your passions: what could you get involved in and where might you add value ? Remember, life isn't all about work.

Work to live, not live to work.

Could you use your skills in a charity or a local organisation where you would feel valued and wanted once you have decided that you can't just work, work and work? People and organisations out there need you, so what have you got to offer?

Outside of work

- What can you get more involved in?
- What hobbies and interests do you enjoy?
- What other activities might you enjoy?
- What else could you do that would involve your passions?
- What is your current level of health and well-being?
- What could you do more of (or differently) to maximise your energy levels in the following areas:

  Exercise / sport / travel/ arts / music / theatre / cinema / history / religion / local community / give something back / classes / night school / Open University / cooking / DIY / build something.

- What skills do you have that local clubs and organisations might be interested in?

A healthy balance outside work often means a more effective person inside work. It can give you a happier, more fulfilled you. It doesn't always just happen though — it needs thought and effort.

If you don't create your ideal lifestyle, who is going to do it for you?

Managing My Finances

Along with the well-being section of this book, there are loads of resources dedicated to the subject of managing your finances. In terms of Future Proofing Yourself, it's worth thinking about your finances along with your skillsets and how employable you are going to be during the rest of your career through into retirement.

I have three very important tips for you to consider.

Tip One

The best way to improve your finances and income is to earn more by developing your skills, knowledge and experiences. The more you can contribute, the more you can earn, and the more value you can bring to your business, the more you will be worth. Again, having transferable skills will make a big difference to your earning potential and marketability.

This is a key message behind Future Proofing Yourself: the more you invest in your skills and your development, the more financially stable you will become.

If we don't invest in ourselves, who is going to do it for us?

Tip Two

As we approach the end of our careers, we need to plan for earning less money. The time to stop and reflect is actually when we are at our peak in terms of earning potential. We need to ask ourselves whether we can realistically maintain this pace and level of earnings until our retirement. Usually the answer is "No."

What is happening in my business that will impact my future learning opportunities? Is it time to accept that I have already maximised my earnings potential and therefore need to make the appropriate changes to my life and spending habits? Think about what financial obligations you might take on after you have hit your peak? Having that conversation with your family is critical. Do you need the added stress of adding to your mortgage or can you now start to enjoy more freedom and less financial burden? Why can't you enjoy what you have and stop chasing the dream? Instead, start living your dream and enjoy it — you have earned it.

Tip Three

Think about all the possessions you have in your home — do you really have to keep it all? Focus upon needs, wants and desires. And prioritise what to keep and what to buy in the future.

- What are the essentials that you need in your home (I.e. the items that you keep and look after)?
- What do you want in your home? Look around you — do you think, "Well I wanted it once, but now it's just clutter; can I sell it and recoup some money?" I would hazard a guess that in the average household we could easily recoup several hundred pounds by selling our clutter.
- Ask yourself before buying any further items that you think you want — is it really worth it? How long will I want it for?
- What do you desire in your home? These are items that bring happiness and make you feel good. Look after them and take care of them. But challenge your purchases, — do they really make you happier? If they do, great, if not, don't buy them.
- Think before you buy. If you cut out the items which only provide you with short-term gratification, you will save a lot of money. Instead, invest in things of quality that you really

desire, or invest in better quality items that you need for your home.

Once you get to a stage in life when you own most things to allow you to live comfortably, try this simple test before buying anything else. If I buy something, what would I get rid of in its place?

This focuses the mind on the rationale behind future purchases. It protects you from short-term impulsive buys and makes you think about what you need and really desire.

Only buy new items either to replace old ones or because doing so will bring you happiness.

If only we could win the lottery – well, you have!

I have a friend who will not like me writing this, but here goes...

He often says "If only..." when he talks about items or investments that he wishes he had bought. He frequently wants to discuss how great it would be if he could buy something he hasn't already got. He is always talking about winning the lottery and wishing for stuff. He lives in a lovely house with a nice car and lots of material things that he enjoys. He often orders brochures of items he would like or sends off for holiday and property particulars and wants to discuss them in detail, but he knows they are out of his current financial reach.

I often say to him, "To the majority of people, when they see your lifestyle and what you have, they think you've won the lottery. There are people who look up to you and think you have a great lifestyle."

Yes, it would be lovely to win the lottery but don't let it consume you, don't torment yourself with, "If only I could buy this or buy that". Would it really make you any happier?

Enjoy what you have got.

If you want something else, make the necessary choices and make it happen. Work hard and go for it but please, stop going on about it!

Creating self-value and purpose

At different times of our career, we often need to create purposes or focuses for our life rather than just work, work and more work.

Creating self-worth and a true sense of purpose outside of work is very good for one's own well-being.

I have often felt women are better at this than men; for example, my wife and her friends are far better at keeping in touch than I am with my friends. They have more hobbies and interests which creates togetherness, support and well-being. They find value and belonging in sharing and self-worth in helping each other out.

Whether it's by choice or by design, women seem to find it easier to cut down on their hours and still possess self-value and worth, which I feel creates a healthier life style.

Naturally a lot of people need to keep working for financial reasons. So how much time do you give to your financial planning in life, something which is just as important as managing your self-development?

Can we learn to create a way of reducing our hours and pay towards the end of our careers by changing our life styles?

It's often called a mid-life crisis. We always dream of success in our careers and our relationships, but what if, for whatever reason, these dreams don't quite play out in real life. We start to become a bit run-down and (as previously discussed) we can soon end up with a nasty surprise when we find out that work isn't going to plan and our services are no longer required.

There is plenty of advice around for the younger generation on how to develop and build their careers and for the older generation on the need to stay active and keeping their minds and bodies fit. However, for people in their middle 30s to late 50s, there isn't much help at all.

Plan in time to think how can you help yourself. Work on your friendship groups, get involved in organisations where you can add value and help such as charities or local organisations in your community. When we hit middle age, we naturally start to worry about slowing down and becoming less attractive to other people. In the context of this book, that means less attractive regarding our employability in the eyes of other companies.

So, whilst ageing can impact our relationships, it can also influence our work and careers given all the responsibilities that we have assumed. Learning to manage and be aware of what is happening to us is very important to ensure that we don't press the wrong buttons and make bad decisions as a consequence. There are no set rules on how to deal with these situations but creating a feeling of purpose and value, along with healthy levels of self-esteem can help us manage the process through our middle age.

Taking plenty of reflection time and investing in doing things that you enjoy and which bring you value and purpose are essential for your own well-being:

- What do you really enjoy doing?
- Can you do more of it?
- How can you get more involved with different organisations and groups?

Chapter Eight: Next Steps Forward

How are you going to make it happen?

Procrastination isn't an option!

Exciting times lie ahead with numerous opportunities and experiences to be explored. Don't be left wondering and thinking, "What if...?" If in doubt, go for it, learn from it and enjoy your journeys.

Generating ideas in your career or making that jump to start your own business can be fun and exciting as well as a bit daunting. You will need help though — don't imagine that you can just take on the whole world on your own. We all have that vision in our minds of a great business idea or what our ideal career would look like. To make that a reality, ask for some honest feedback on your ideas, do your research, trial it out, give it a go... but don't be left thinking, "What I was going to do was..." and regret that you never got round to it.

Discuss your career ideas with experienced people in your network and decide either, "Yes, let's crack on", or "No, I don't want to do that" and obtain closure. Make a decision so you don't retire thinking to yourself, "What I should have done was..."

Your network is very important to you. Manage it, use it to help others and have great conversations to help each other out. Use your network to help you make a decision, obtain feedback and solicit honest advice.

Whichever way your career takes you and whatever decisions you make, work hard to make it happen and be enthusiastic about yourself. You are the one that needs to sell 'you' and make things happen, so if you can't be positive about yourself, you can't expect other people to be.

Performing to the best of your abilities is one of the most important principles of Future Proofing Yourself. Be a great performer in your area of expertise. If you are going to try and do anything in life, give it a go, a really good go. Make decisions and make your ideas work. Get organised and focused — don't spend your time wondering, "What if... ?", or "I should have..."

Key principles behind 'Giving it a Go'

- Being very organised and focused.
- Making decisions and making things happen.
- Reflecting often on your experiences and future plans.
- Upskill and be constantly learning.
- Managing your network.
- Working on the way you think.
- Working hard to make things happen and performing to the best of your abilities.
- Enjoying your journey and being happy.

"Being happy and content is a great sign of success"

We can do all the reflecting, planning, thinking and conversations we like, but there comes a time when action is required. Nobody else is going to do it for you — it's time for you to make that phone call, sign up for that course, make that decision, or have that conversation. It's now time for action!

Remember if you don't make it happen for you, who is going to do it for you?

Creating work ideas

Wouldn't it be great if I could...? Well, why don't I?!

The key to generating ideas for business is not to evaluate them too quickly. Statements such as, "That won't work", or "We've tried that before", as soon as somebody comes up with an initial idea or concept aren't very helpful; they will deter people from being creative and developing other follow-on ideas.

Speak to like-minded people in your network to test your ideas. Try to promote informal conversations rather than set meetings with agendas. Go for a coffee, for lunch or find a different environment.

I used to take people who I was coaching to a certain art gallery in London where we ended up discussing all sorts of things to help them open up and think differently. It certainly worked when it came to generating different ways of thinking. We would often have random conversations regarding a certain piece of art or a particular picture and then suddenly, the person I was coaching would exclaim, "That's given me a great idea!" We would then explore that idea but be careful not to evaluate it.

Being creative and thinking of work innovations can be very tough in an office environment. Try to go on trips round customer sites or supplier's factories, where you can talk to different people and obtain a different perspective on your business.

I consider myself very lucky in my work. I get to visit lots of different companies and tour round them, meeting all sorts of different people. It always helps me to think differently as well as understand their needs better. Plus, I find that I get into interesting small talk conversations which help me to generate different ideas and conversations, something which I'd never get in a meeting room or a video conferencing call.

Talk to people in different industries and be inquisitive. Look at your network and at who has an interesting working environment which you could visit. Let them do the talking. Remember you know how you think and what you think; learn from others and from their ideas. Be good at opening people up with great questions on their thoughts and ideas, or on how their businesses work. Discuss with key maverick owners or directors of businesses about how they work and operate. I love those conversations. All that free learning, ideas and information.

If you can secure a one-to-one with a business owner, grab the opportunity. Learn from them and be prepared to ask some great questions. I usually like to ask them about their story and how they made certain crucial decisions, as well as how the see their markets developing in the future.

I find travelling a great way to think creatively, be it by trains, airplanes or boat (but don't forget to turn your phone off!) However, I struggle to think differently when I'm driving, as I find I have to concentrate hard on the road. Many people I talk to say they find it easy to think whilst driving, although when I ask them whether they can recall their journey to work, they usually reply, "No". Not so good on the Health & Safety front then!

Work hard at generating ideas and invest your time wisely. Don't use the common excuse , "But I'm too busy", since you will be the one who will benefit from new ideas and learning from others.

Working for myself

Being your own boss. For some people, it's all they have ever wanted, although many people say they want to be their own boss but never actually do anything about it. On the other hand, others hate the thought of being their own boss and much prefer the security of employment (although as we have already seen, there are no guarantees on this front anymore). We are all different in our own unique ways; there is no right or wrong when it comes to thinking about whether you should work for yourself or not.

So, if do you like the idea of being your own boss, the big question is, "Where do I start?" There is a wealth of advice and opinion out there but remember to question whether your business will be sustainable and whether there will be a market for your idea until you finish work and retire.

Working for yourself and becoming your own boss might represent a brilliant transition to slowly cutting back on your working hours and improving your work:life balance. However, it will need plenty of discipline to make sure you don't end up doing even more hours!

So, four really important questions:

1. Do you have enough passion and drive to succeed in making your idea happen?
2. Is there a sustainable market to enable you to make a good profit / get a decent return for all the hours that you are going to invest?
3. How will you source new business and deal with rejection?
4. What skills, knowledge and experience do you have to make your business work?

I have spoken with lots of people who have started up on their own. Technically, they are usually great at what they do, with a great passion and desire for their work. But (and it is a big BUT), is there a profitable marketplace for their product or service and how will they make sales and a profit? These are really important questions that need very careful consideration.

Fortunately, I come from a sales environment and am very disciplined in my sales and networking activities.

- Be prepared to work very hard and to focus upon activities that generate sales.
- Learn how to promote and sell yourself and your business.
- Have lots of passion and love for what you do.
- Use your network and people you trust for honest feedback (which will save you a lot of money and plenty of heartache).

When deciding to be your own boss, remember: nothing ventured, nothing gained. If in doubt, give it a go, but don't jump in without doing your research first and being positive about your decision. Above all, don't look back when you are 70 years old and say to yourself, "I wish I had..."

Which way next?

Times change, we change, our motivations change and, sometimes, our values change. You have obviously done a great job so far in your career and perhaps now you need a new journey or challenge, but you have got to enjoy it.

If you can afford to enjoy what you have done and you can let go, move on to the next chapter in your life and your career.

It's all about making the right choices at the right time. There is no book saying you must do this or that; go with the flow of what you think is right for you. Changing jobs and especially careers isn't always as easy as it sounds; do your homework and ask your network for advice and listen. If in doubt, go for it and learn from the experience.

Create reflection time and employ the tried and trusted technique of looking at the positives and negatives behind making any changes before going off in a new direction. Think of it like going horse racing and expecting to lose, say £100. At the end of the day, you should be able to think to yourself, “Well, I had a great day out”, rather than “Damn, I just lost £100!” or that you should just have stayed at home and been bored.

So, if you want an adventure and want to try something new, be aware of the pitfalls first, so at least in the future you can look back and say, “Yes, but I gave it a good go.”

Don’t do it half-heartedly or keep saying “What I want to do”; go and give it everything and enjoy the journey, confident that you have made the right choice for you. Always try to look back and say, “I made the choices and the decisions; the journey had some ups and downs, but I gave it a go”. Think “Good on me!”

Be a great performer

It sounds obvious and it is; you can do all the planning, networking and strategising that you want, but at the end of the day, you have got to be really good at what you do.

I once went to a Speaker’s Conference and one of the presenters absolutely nailed it. He spoke at length about how he had sat through lots of talks at the conference and had heard how to:

- Sell himself to clients;
- Write great profiles;
- Have a top website;
- Have brilliant LinkedIn and Facebook pages;
- Develop great Twitter posts;

- Have cool visuals on his PowerPoint slides;
- Be great at networking;
- Etc...

However, he then said: "That's all great and the topics mentioned here can help you along your way, but the best thing you can do for yourself is to deliver a great talk or speech. Go and knock your audiences socks off!"

It is very true; we all need to perform to the best of our abilities and be very good at what we do. People will then want to work with us and have us working for them.

Be great at what you do; be calm, focused and self-aware of the impact you have on yourself and others. Practice your skills, both technical and non-technical, solicit feedback and work hard at being good at what you do.

Give it everything. As Usain Bolt said after 2008 Olympics where he won 3 gold medals and broke three world records, he gave it everything and performed to the best of his abilities. You can't do much more than that. Give it everything you have.

Be a great version of yourself, maximise your potential and your opportunities.

After all, if you don't do it for you, who is going to do it for you?

Professional Responsibility

We all might like to think we are professional in our work and that we are a great investment for the companies we work for, but do we always demonstrate professional responsibility in our everyday work?

Do you wake up in the morning and think, "I am going to be really good today — I'm going to show how good I am." Do you see your work as a challenge to allow you to develop and learn more, so that you can enjoy what you do, stay relevant and be of great value to the organisation that you work for (or to your clients if you work for yourself)?

Taking professional responsibility and self-managing yourself is the height of professionalism —this is something which we expect from people in the public eye, be it in the sporting world or the world of entertainment. We are paid to do a job, but do we always perform to the best of our abilities, demonstrating the right attitudes and skills? If not, then why not?

Being the best that you can be will help safeguard your future career, learning and developing as you go, constantly reflecting to make sure you are on the right track.

Future Proofing Yourself covers many aspects of your working life and the need to continuously develop and improve your skills to keep yourself relevant and of value for the rest of your career. You will experience highs and lows during your working lives, but what is most important is how you react and manage the different situations and challenges that you encounter.

Above all, life is about enjoying yourself. We all have to spend rather a lot of our time working (for obvious reasons) but enjoying what you do should be high on your aspirations list, because if you feel happy in your working life, you will be able to enjoy other aspects of your life. You will feel fulfilled and contented, which is important to most of us.

I have tried to cover what I feel are the key areas that we as individuals need to focus on in order to Future Proof Ourselves. These areas will differ depending upon the occupation or the job, but they will all require constant development, reflection and self-learning. A lot of the ideas, skills and techniques require a level of determination and hard work to make sure that these new behaviours become long-term habits.

But remember above all, "If you don't look after yourself, who is going to do it for you?"

Enjoy your journey.

Please do let me know how you get on.

David

Future Proofing Yourself

Reflections Document

Please create some reflection time to sit, read and ponder the questions below regarding your own self-development.

You don't have to answer all of the questions – it's not a test after all. You may feel that some aren't relevant or appropriate — if that's the case, simply move on to the next one. However, some questions might encourage you to explore yourself further in ways that you hadn't previously considered.

Just create some time for you and give your mind and inner thoughts a bit of a workout.

Write down at the back of your notebook some of the key questions that you would like to work on. Alternatively, add them to a notes page on your mobile device or create a document on your laptop so that you can reflect on them on a regular basis.

Invest in yourself – if you don't who is going to do it for you?

REFLECTIONS, CHAPTER ONE: A TIME TO REFLECT?

- What do you enjoy the most about your work?
- What do you **not** enjoy about your work?
- What are your natural strengths?
- What are you passionate about?
- What hidden talents do you have that you feel are underutilised?
- What Is your definition of success?
- What would you like to create or develop for yourself and those closest to you?
- What would you describe as your biggest weakness?
- What advice would you give somebody in the same situation as you to help develop their potential and maximise opportunities that are put before them?
- How can you take more self-responsibility in managing your own appraisal process and self-development plans for the future?
- Would you want to work with 'you'? And why?
- If you have management responsibilities, would you want 'you' as your manager? And why?

REFLECTIONS, CHAPTER TWO: PERSONAL DEVELOPMENT AND MAXIMISING OPPORTUNITIES

If in Doubt, Go for It

- What is really important to you as a person?
- What personal values are important to you?
- What gives you real purpose and meaning and makes you feel fulfilled and good about yourself?
- What really motivates you? (If you already have plenty of money, think a bit deeper).
- What is your personal mission in life?
- Where do you see yourself in five years' time?
- What are the first steps you might need to take to get you there?

REFLECTIONS, CHAPTER THREE: ANTICIPATING CHANGE IN YOUR WORKING WORLD

Build awareness and take responsibility

- What changes do you see on the horizon in your working environment?
- What social trends may have an impact?
- What political, legal or economic trends may drive changes in your organisation?
- What technological developments may drive changes to your ways of working?

Career Changes

- Realistically describe your ideal job or career
- Why is this your ideal job or career and what unique skills do you possess which could make this happen?
- What interests you or where do you feel 'in flow'?
- Who could you talk to regarding their job or career to source ideas?
- Do you consider career progression as an upwards move or a sideways / lateral move? What lateral move may be of interest?
- Does fear of the unknown hold you back?
- If 'yes', what are you afraid might happen?
- How likely is this to happen?
- What could you do to avoid / be prepared for this?

REFLECTIONS, CHAPTER FOUR: MANAGING YOUR KEY SKILL SETS

What do you need to do to keep ahead of the game?

- What has gone well for you recently that has given you extra confidence?
- What makes you unique?
- What are your key strengths in your current role?
- How do you demonstrate that you are flexible and agile in your working environment?
- What opportunities do you have to maximise your potential?
- How do you create reflection time for yourself to think about key areas of your work and life?
- How frequently do you reflect on the above? Is this enough, if not, how could you ensure that you reflect more often?
- How regularly do you review whether you are meeting your targets and achieving your personal goals?
- Is this often enough and if not, how could you ensure that you do this more frequently?
- Identify the key people with whom you need to make a greater impact in your working environment.
- What influences them and how do they make decisions?

Managing Your Self Development

- What have you learnt about yourself recently?
- Do you prefer to stay within your comfort zone?

- When have you been outside your comfort zone recently? What did you learn about yourself?
- What opportunities do you have on the horizon that will encourage you to move outside your comfort zone?
- What personal qualities or attributes do you need to develop in order to improve or to progress in your career?
- What knowledge or skills do you need to develop?
- What new experiences do you feel a need to gain and how can you obtain those experiences?

Opportunities to learn – Go Grab an experience

- What stops you from embarking on skills development?
- What kind of learning do you prefer – on-line, self-paced, classroom or one-to-one?

Key skills and competences for your future

- What inter-personal skills (communication, confidence and other 'soft skills') do you see as being important in order to meet changing requirements?
    - Leadership / Management
    - Negotiation and influencing
    - Team building
    - Customer Service
    - Planning
    - Time Management
- What technical skills do you (or might you) need to develop?
    - IT skills – Microsoft / use of CRM packages
    - Digital marketing / social media

REFLECTIONS, CHAPTER FIVE: PROACTIVE SELF-MANAGEMENT

If you don't look after yourself, who will?

- Set and manage personal and career goals

	PERSONAL	WORK
Short-term		
Medium-term		
Long-term		

- Do you feel fulfilled in your current position? If not, what would make you feel more fulfilled?
- What causes you worry or concern?
- What are the things which you can control?
- What are the things which you cannot control but which you could learn to think about from a different perspective? (If you don't like something, change the way you think about it).
- How can you create the right mind-set for you?
- Keeping the focus on the right things — what's important to you?

- What can you do for yourself to be more organised and get more things done; i.e. to be more effective and efficient.
- How well do you manage your time?
- How good are you at prioritising? How could you improve this?
- Do you switch between tasks constantly or complete one task before tackling the next?
- If you switch frequently, what could you do to increase the time you are focusing on an individual task without interruption?
- Do you thrive on 'being busy'? If so, what could you usefully 'let go'?
- Do you find it difficult to say 'No'? What is stopping you? What could you do differently?

REFLECTIONS, CHAPTER SIX: DEVELOPING A CLEVER WAY OF THINKING

Networking opportunities

- Who do you need to know better in your business i.e. people to connect with / business partners?
- When networking, what is your 'Call to Action'?
- Who do you need to build a relationship with outside your business and why?
- Who can help you in your career? Friends, family or a work mentor?
- Who would be good to keep in contact with — old colleagues, friends from school, higher education, university?
- How frequently do you purposefully spend time networking to expand your exposure in your working world? Would you benefit from increasing the time spent on this? What opportunities are available to you?
- Who inspires you?
- 'Who' helps you to think differently and why?
- 'What' helps you to think differently and why?
- 'Where' helps you to think differently and why?

REFLECTIONS, CHAPTER SEVEN: BEING IN CONTROL OF YOUR WELL-BEING

- What hobbies and interests do you enjoy?
- What other activities might you enjoy?
- What else could you do that would spark your passions?
- What is your current level of health and well-being?
- What could you do more of or differently to maximise your energy levels in the following areas:
    - Exercise & Sport
    - Eating & Drinking (Nutrition)
    - Sleep
    - Time for family and friends

REFLECTIONS, CHAPTER EIGHT: NEXT STEPS FORWARD

How are you going to make it happen?

- After completing this reflection document what will you now go and do for 'you'?

Enjoy your Journey

If in doubt, give it a go and go for it!

BV - #0007 - 210420 - C0 - 210/148/12 - PB - 9781912243853